G. T. HAWKER

The Mini
OXFORD

School
Speller

Oxford University Press

Contents

Instructions

1   Think hard about the word you wish to spell and try to decide with which two letters it starts.

2   Find these two letters in the Index and you will see the number of the page where the word can be found or where you should begin looking for it.

3   Turn to this page and look down the column under these two letters until you find the word you want. Where there are a lot of words which begin with the same two letters, the first three letters of the words are given at the top of the column to help you find the word you want.

It may be necessary to add the word endings shown on the right-hand side of the column in order to build up the complete word you want, e.g.

rich   er, est, ly, ness, es
hair   dresser, -dryer, pin, -slide, -style, s

Here the words **richer, richest, richly, richness** and **riches** may be built up, and also **hairdresser(s), hair-dryer(s), hairpin(s), hair-slide(s), hair-style(s)** and **hairs**.

Where the last letter or letters of a word are in a lighter print these must be left off before adding to the other endings, e.g.

happy   ier, iest, ily, iness

Here the y must be left off before making:

happier, happiest, happily, happiness.

The plurals of most nouns may be formed by adding the letter, or letters, shown in lighter print on the extreme right of the column. A few nouns have their plurals given in full on the right of the column, and you will notice that some nouns have two plurals, either of which may be used, e.g. **cactuses** or **cacti, hoofs** or **hooves, fish** or **fishes.**

All the words with ed, ing after them are verbs or may be used as verbs. If you require the word to end in either ed or ing, remember the following:

(a) **kick**   ed, ing, s =
     kicked   kicking   kicks

Here ed or ing or s may be added to the verb without changing the word at all.

(b) **stab**   bed, bing, s =
     stabbed   stabbing   stabs
     stop   ped, ping, s =
     stopped   stopping   stops

Here you can see that the final consonant (the last

letter) of these verbs has to be doubled before adding ed or ing.

(c) **blame**   d, ¢ing, s   =
    blamed blaming blames

Where a verb ends in a letter **e** the d or s may be added to the word but the **e** must be dropped before adding ing. An ¢ is placed before the ing to remind you of this.

There are a few other verbs which change their endings in different ways. You will usually find these endings printed by the side of, above or below, the verb, e.g.

began		**lie** d, s	**carry** ing
begin	ning, s	**lying**	**carried** ies
begun			

Warning: A word which has a star (*) after it has the same sound, or almost the same sound, as another word; but it has a different meaning and spelling, e.g. **knew* new*; their* there*; which* witch***. The word endings will help you to decide which of these words you want and so will the words in brackets. These are included to guide you; they are not always exact definitions. The words are paired in small print at the bottom of the page. If you find that you have looked up the wrong word you may easily see how the other is spelt and where it may be found in its correct alphabetical place in the book.

ab	
ab	
abandon	ed, ing, ment, s
abate	d, ing, ment, s
abbess	es
abbey	s
abbot	s
abduct	ed, ing, ion, s
abhor	red, ring, rence, rent, s
abide	d, ing, s
ability	ies
ablaze	
able	r, st, –bodied
abnormal	ity, ly
aboard	
abolish	ed, ing, es
abominable	
abominate	d, ing, s
Aboriginal	
Aborigines	s or **Aborigines**
abound	ed, ing, s

ac	
ac	
academy	ies
accelerate	d, ing, s
accent	s
accept* (receive)	able, ed, ing, s
accident	al, ally, s
accommodate	d, ing, s
accommodation	
accompany	ing
accompanied	ies
accomplish	ed, ing, es
according	ly
account	ed, ing, ant, s
accumulate	d, ing, s
accuracy	
accurate	ly
accusation	s
accuse	d, ing, s
accustom	ed, ing, s

about	
above	-board
abreast	
abroad	ly, ness
abrupt	es
abscess	
absence	ed, ing, ly, ee, s
absent	s
absent-minded	ly, ness
absolute	ly
absorb	ed, ing, ent, s
abstain	ed, ing, s
absurd	ity, ly
abundance	
abundant	ly
abuse	d, éing, s
abysmal	ly
abyss	es

ache	d, éing, s
achieve	d, éing, ment, s
acid	s
acknowledge	d, éing, s
acknowledg(e)ment	s
acorn	s
acquaint	ed, ing, ance, s
acquire	d, éing, ment, s
acre	age, s
acrobat	ic, s
across	
act	ed, ing, s
actor	s
actress	es
action	s
active	ly
activity	ies
actual	ly

é Drop **e** before adding **ing**

* accept
   except

ad

ae af ag

ae			
aerial	s		
aerodrome	s		
aeronaut	ic, s		
aeroplane	s		
af			
affair			
affect	ed, ing, s		
affection	s		
affectionate	ly, ness		
affix	ed, ing, es		
afford	ed, ing, s		
afloat			
afraid			
after			
afternoon			
afterwards	s		

ad	
adapt	able, ed, ing, or, s
add	ed, ing, s
addition	al, s
adder	s
address	ed, ing, es
adequate	ly
adhere	d, éing, s
adhesive	s
adjective	s
adjoin	ed, ing, s
adjust	able, ed, ing, ment, s
admirable	y
admiral	s
admiration	
admire	d, éing, r, s
admission	s
admit	ted, ting, s
admittance	

adopt	ed, ing, ion, s	**ag**	
adorable	y		
adore	d, e̸ing, s	**again**	
adorn	ed, ing, ment, s	**against**	
adrift		**age**	d, less, -group, s
adult	s	**agent**	s
advance	d, e̸ing, ment, s	**ageing** or **aging**	
advantage	s	**aggravate**	d, e̸ing, s
adventure	d, e̸ing, r, s	**aggressive**	ly, ness
adventurous	ly, ness	**aghast**	
adverb	s	**agile**	ly
adversary	ies	**agility**	ies
advertise	d, e̸ing, r, s	**agitate**	d, e̸ing, s
advertisement	s	**ago**	
advice		**agonize**	d, e̸ing, s
advisable		**agony**	ies
advise	d, e̸ing, r, s	**agree**	able, d, ing, ment, s
advocate	d, e̸ing, s	**agriculture**	
		aground	al

e̸ Drop e before adding ing

ai

aid	ed, ing, s
ail* (be ill)	ed, ing, ment, s
aim	ed, ing, less, lessly, s
air*	ed, ing, crew, mail, tight, man
air*	men, gun, field, line, port, way, s
aircraft	-carrier
Airedale	s
air force	s
airy	ier, iest, ily, iness
aisle* (part of a church; gangway)	s

al

alarm	ed, ing, ist, -bell, -clock, s
album	s
alcohol	ism, ic, s
alcove	s
ale* (beer)	s

am

alphabet	ical, ically, s
already	
Alsatian	s
also	
altar* (church table)	s
alter* (change)	ed, ing, ation, s
alternate	d, ing, ly, s
alternative	ly, s
although	
altitude	
altogether	
aluminium	
always	

am

amateur	ish, s
amaze	d, ing, ment, s
amber	

alert	ed, ing, ly, ness, s
algebra	
alibi	s
alien	s
alight	ed, ing, s
alike	
alive	
all right	
alley	way, s
alligator	s
allot	ted, ting, ment, s
allow	ed,* ing, ance, s
ally	ies
almond	-blossom, -paste, -tree, s
almost	
alone	
along	side
aloud* (loudly)	

ambition	s
ambitious	ly, ness
amble	d, *e*ing, s
ambulance	man, men, s
ambush	ed, ing, es
amend	ed, ing, ment, s
amiable	y
amid or **amidst**	
amiss	
ammunition	
among or **amongst**	
amount	ed, ing, s
amphibian	s or **amphibia**
amphibious	ly
ample	r, st, ness
amplifier	s
amputate	d, *e*ing, s
amuse	d, *e*ing, s

ail   ale   *

air   heir

aisle   isle

allowed   aloud

altar   alter

e Drop **e** before adding *ing*

an	
anaesthetic	s
ancestor	s
ancestry	ies
anchor	ed, ing, age, s
ancient	ly, ness, s
anemone	s
angel	s
anger	ed, ing, s
angry	ier, iest, ily
angle	d, ɖing, r, s
anguish	ed, ing, es
animal	s
ankle	s
anniversary	ies
announce	d, ɖing, r, ment, s
annoy	ed, ing, ance, s
annual	ly, s
anoint	ed, ing, ment, s

ap	
apart	
apartment	s
ape	d, ɖing, s
apiary	ies
apiece	
apologetic	al, ally
apologize	d, ɖing, s
apology	ies
apostle	s
appal	led, ling, lingly, s
apparatus	es or **apparatus**
apparent	ly
appeal	ed, ing, ingly, s
appear	ed, ing, ance, s
appendicitis	
appetite	s
appetizing	ly
applaud	ed, ing, s

anonymous	ly
anorak	s
another	
answer	ed, ing, s
ant	-eater, -hill, s
antarctic	
antelope	s
antic	s
anticipate	d, éing, s
anticipation	s
antique	-dealer, -shop, s
antirrhinum	s
antiseptic	s
antler	s
anvil	s
anxiety	ies
anxious	ly
any	body, one, how, thing, way, where

applause	
apple	-core, -pie, -sauce, -tart, -tree, s
appliance	s
applicant	s
application	s
apply	ing
applied	ies
appoint	ed, ing, ment, s
appreciate	d, éing, s
appreciation	s
apprentice	d, éing, ship, s
approach	ed, ing, es
approval	s
approve	d, éing, s
approximate	ly, d, éing, s
apricot	s
April	
apron	s

aq ar

as

aq

aquarium	s or aquaria
aquatic	s
aqueduct	s

ar

arable	
arc* (curve)	-lamp, -light, s
arcade	s
arch	ed, ing, es
archway	s
archaeological	ly
archaeologist	s
archaeology	
archer	y, s
architect	ure, ural, s
arctic	
are	

array	ed, ing, s
arrest	ed, ing, s
arrival	s
arrive	d, ∉ing, s
arrow	-head, s
arsenic	
art	work, s
artist	ic, ically, s
artful	ly, ness
artery	ies
article	s
artificial	ity, ly, ness
artillery	man, men

as

ascend	ed, ing, s
ascent	s
ascertain	ed, ing, s

aren't (are not)	
area	s
arena	s
argue	d, ~~e~~ing, s
argument	s
arise	n, ~~e~~ing, s
arithmetic	al
ark* (boat; box)	s
arm	ed, ing, band, chair, ful, hole, pit, s
armada	s
armament	s
armistice	s
armour	ed, y, -plated, -plating
army	ies
arose	
around	
arouse	d, ~~e~~ing, s
arrange	d, ~~e~~ing, r, ment, s

*   arc
     ark

ash	en, y, es
ashamed	
ashore	
aside	
ask	ed, ing, s
asleep	
asparagus	
asphyxiate	d, ~~e~~ing, s
aspirin	s
ass	es
assail	ed, ing, ant, s
assassin	ation, s
assassinate	d, ~~e~~ing, s
assault	ed, ing, s
assemble	d, ~~e~~ing, s
assembly	ies
assist	ed, ing, ance, s
assistant	s

~~e~~ Drop e before adding ing

at

associate	d, ∉ing, s
association	s
assort	ed, ing, ment, s
assume	d, ∉ing, s
assure	d, ∉ing, s
aster	s
asthma	tic, tical
astonish	ed, ing, es, ment
astound	ed, ing, s
astray	
astride	
astrologer	s
astrology	ical
astronaut	s
astronomer	s
astronomy	ical
asylum	s

au av

attic	s
attitude	s
attract	ed, ing, ion, s
attractive	ly, ness
attribute	d, ∉ing, s

au

auburn	
auction	ed, ing, eer, s
audible	
audience	s
audition	ed, ing, s
August	
aunt	s
aunties or **aunt**y	ies
author	s
authoress	es
authority	ies

at	
ate* (eat)	
athlete	s
athletic	ally, s
Atlantic	
atlas	es
atmosphere	es
atom	ic, -bomb, s
atrocious	ly, ness
attach	ed, ing, able, es
attachment	s
attack	ed, ing, er; s
attain	ed, ing, able, ment, s
attempt	ed, ing, s
attend	ed, ing, ance, s
attendant	s
attention	s
attentive	ly, ness

authorize	d, éing, s
autobiography	ical, ies
autograph	ed, ing, s
automatic	ally
automation	
autumn	al, s
av	
available	s
avalanche	s
avenge	d, éing, r; s
avenue	s
average	d, éing, s
aviary	ies
aviation	
aviator	s
avoid	ed, ing, able, ance, s

é Drop e before adding ing

* ate
* eight (8)

aw

await	ed, ing, s
awake	d, d̸ing, s
awaken	ed, ing, s
award	ed, ing, s
aware	ness
away	
awe	some, struck, stricken
awful	ly, ness
awhile	
awkward	ly, ness
awning	s
awoke or awaked	
awry	

ax

axe	d, d̸ing, -blade, -handle, s
axis	es
axle	s

ba

baggy	ier; iest; ily, iness
bagpipe	s
bail* (wicket cross-piece)	s
bait	ed, ing, s
bake	d, d̸ing, r, house, s
bakery	ies
balance	d, d̸ing; r; s
balcony	ies
bald	ing, er; est, ly, ness, -headed
bale* (bundle)	d, d̸ing; r; s
bale* {out of plane or throw out water	d, d̸ing; r; s
ball*	-game, point, -pen, room; s
ballast	s
ballerina	s
ballet	-dancing, -dancer, -shoe, s
balloon	ed, ing, ist; s
ballot	ed, ing, -paper; s
bamboo	s

ba	

babe	s
baboon	s
baby	ies
bachelor	s
back	ed, ing, cloth, ground, yard, s
backward	ly, ness, s
bacon	
bad	-tempered, ly, ness
badge	ed, ing, s
badger	-racket
badminton	
baffle	d, é'ing, s
bag	ged, ging, ful, -snatcher, s
baggage	

ban	ned, ning, s
banana	s
band	ed, ing, sman, smen, stand, s
bandage	d, é'ing, s
bandit	s
bang	ed, ing, er, s
bangle	s
banish	ed, ing, es, ment
banister	s
banjo	es or s
bank	ed, ing, er, -book, note, s
bankrupt	ed, ing, s, cy
banner	s
banquet	ed, ing, s
bantam	s
baptism	s
baptize	d, é'ing, s
bar	red, ring, maid, s

é' Drop e before adding ing

ball	ball
* bale	bawl

be

barbecue	d, éing, s
barbed	-wire
barber	s
bare* (naked; empty)	ly, ness, d, éing, s
bargain	ed, ing, er; s
barge	d, éing, e, -pole, s
bark	ed, ing, er; s
barley	corn, -sugar, -water; s
barn	-dance, -owl, yard, s
barnacle	s
barometer	s
baron* (lord)	et; s
barrack	ed, ing, er; -room, -square, s
barrel	ful, s
barren* (bare; empty)	ly, ness
barricade	d, éing, s
barrier	s
barrister	s
barrow	-boy; s

battle	d, éing, axe, field, ship, s
bawl* (shout; cry out)	ed, ing, s
bay	-window, s
bayonet	ed, ing, s
bazaar	s

be

beach* (seashore)	ed, ing, es
beacon	s
bead	ed, ing, work, s
beak	s
beaker	s
beam	ed, ing, s
bean* (plant)	-bag, pole, stalk, s
bear* (carry; endure)	able, ing, er; s
bear* (animal)	skin, s
beard	ed, s
beast	s

barter	d, ing, er, s
base	d, éing, r, st, ly, less, ness, -line, s
baseball	s
basement	s
bash	ed, ing, es
bashful	ly, ness
basin	s
bask	ed, ing, s
basket	ball, ful, s
bat	ted, ting, sman, smen, s
batch	es
bath	ed, ing, mat, robe, room, room, -water, s
bathe	d, éing, r, s
bathing-costume	s
baton	s
battalion	s
batter	ed, ing, s
battery	ies

beastly	ier, iest, iness
beat* (hit; defeat)	en, ing, er, s
beautiful	ly
beauty	ies
beaver	s
became	
because	
beckon	ed, ing, s
become	éing, s
bed	ded, ding, clothes, side, time, room, s
bee	hive, line, keeper, s
beech* (tree)	es
beef	burger, eater, steak, s
been* (past of be)	
beer	y, -barrel, -bottle, -can, s
beet* (vegetable)	root, s
beetle	s
before	hand

é Drop e before adding ing

*	bare	bawl	beach	bean	beat
	bear	ball	beech	been	beet
	baron				
	barren				

bi

Bible	s
bicker	ed, ing, s
bicycle	d, éing, -clip, -pump, s
bid	ding, der, s
bide	d, éing, s
big	ger, gest, ness
bike	d, éing, s
bikini	s
bilberry	ies
bilge	-water, -pump, s
bilious	ly, ness
bill	ed, ing, s
billet	ed, ing, s
billiard	-ball, -cue, -room, -table, s
billion	s
billow	ed, ing, s
bind	ing, er, s
bingo	-hall, s

beg	ged, ging, s
beggar	ly, s
began	
begin	ning, ner, s
begun	
begone	
behave	d, éing, s
behaviour	
behead	ed, ing, s
behind	
being	hand
belief	s
believe	d, éing, r, s
bell	-ringer, tent, -tower, s
bellow	ed, ing, er, s
belong	ed, ing, s
below	
belt	ed, ing, s
bench	es

bend	ing, er; s		**binoculars**	
bent			**biography**	ical, ies
beneath			**biology**	ical, ist
benefit	ed, ing, s		**biped**	s
benevolent	ly		**birch**	es
beret* (cap)	s		**bird**	-bath, -cage, -seed, -table, s
berry* (fruit)	ies		**birth*** (born)	day, mark, place, rate, s
berth* (bunk; moor a ship)	ed, ing, s		**biscuit**	s
beside	s		**bisect**	ed, ing, ion, s
besiege	d, ȼing, r; s		**bishop**	s
best			**bison**	**bison**
bet	ted, ting, ter; s		**bit**	ty; s
betray	al, ed, ing, er; s		**bitch**	es
better	ed, ing, s		**bite**	ȼing, r; s
between			**bitten**	
beware			**bitter**	er, est, ly, ness
bewilder	ed, ing, ment, s		**bittern**	s
beyond			**bivouac**	ked, king, s

ȼ Drop **e** before adding **ing**

* beret	berth
berry	birth
bury	

bl

black	ed, ing, er, est, ness, smith, s
black	-beetle, bird, board, -currant, s
blackberry	ing
blackberried	ies
blacken	ed, ing, s
blackmail	ed, ing, er, s
blade	d, s
blame	d, *d*ing, less, s
blancmange	s
blank	ed, ing, er, est, ly, ness, s
blanket	s
blare	d, *d*ing, s
blast	ed, ing, s
blaze	d, *d*ing, s
blazer	s
bleach	ed, ing, es
bleak	er, est, ly, ness
bleat	ed, ing, s

bo

blot	ted, ting, ter, s
blouse	s
blow	n, ing, y, er, lamp, pipe, s
blue*(colour)*	r, st, ness, bell, bottle, s
blunder	ed, ing, s
blunt	ed, ing, er, est, ly, ness, s
blush	ed, ing, es
bluster	ed, ing, y, s

bo

boar*(male pig)*	s
board*(wood; ship; lodge)*	ed, ing, s
boarder*(one who boards; lodger)*	s
boast	ed, ing, er, s
boastful	ly, ness
boat	ed, ing, er, man, men, -race, s
bob	bed, bing, -sleigh, s
body	ies

bleed	ing, s
bled	
blend	ed, ing, er, s
bless	ed, ing, ings, es
blew* (blow)	
blind	ed, ing, er, est, ly, ness, s
blindfold	ed, ing, s
blind-man's-buff	
blink	ed, ing, er, s
blister	ed, ing, s
blizzard	s
block	age, ed, ing, s
blockade	d, ɇing, s
blond (masc.)	er, est, s
blonde (fem.)	r, st, s
blood	hound, shed, -stained, thirsty, y
bloom	ed, ing, s
blossom	ed, ing, s

bog	ged, ging, s
boggy	ier, iest, iness
boil	ed, ing, er, s
boisterous	ly, ness
bold	er,* est, ly, ness
bolt	ed, ing, s
bomb	ed, ing, er, -proof, shell, sight, s
bombard	ed, ing, ment, s
bone	d, ɇing, ɇy, -idle, -dry, -shaker, s
bonfire	s
bonnet	s
bonny	ier, iest, ily, iness
book	ed, ing, case, let, seller, stall, s
booking office	s
boom	ed, ing, s
boot	ed, ing, lace, s
border* (edge)	ed, ing, er, less, line, s
bore* (drill hole; weary)	d,* ɇing, dom, s

ɇ Drop e before adding ing

blew			
blue			
*			

boar	board	boarder	bolder
bore	bored	border	boulder

bra

born* (birth)	
borne* (carried)	
borrow	ed, ing, er, s
boss	ed, ing, es
bossy	ier, iest, ily, iness
botany	ical, ist
both	
bother	ed, ing, some, s
bottle	d, ƒing, -opener, s
bottom	ed, ing, less, s
bough* (branch)	
bought* (buy)	
boulder* (large rock)	s
bounce	d, ƒing, r, s
bound	ed, ing, less, s
boundary	ies
bouquet	s
bow* (bend)	ed, ing, s
bow	man, men, shot, string, -tie, s

bre bri

brake* (to stop)	d, ƒing, s
bramble	s
branch	ed, ing, es
brand	ed, ing, -new, s
brandish	ed, ing, es
brandy	ies
brass	es
brave	d, ƒing, r, st, ly, s
bravery	
bravo	s
brawl	ed, ing, er, s
brawn	
brawny	ier, iest, iness
brazen	ed, ing, ly, ness
brazier	s
bread*	-bin, -board, -sauce, -crumb, s
breadth	s
break*	able, age, ing, er, -down, water, s
breakfast	ed, ing, -table, -room, s

bowl	ed, ing, er, s	breast	ed, ing, plate, -stroke, s
bowl	ful, s	breath	less, lessly, -taking, s
box	ed, ing, es	breathe	d, ∉ing, r, s
boxer	s	bred* (brought-up)	
Boxing Day		breed	ing, er, s
boy* (lad)	ish, hood, -friend, s	breeze	
Boy Scout	s	breezy	ier, iest, ily, iness
		brew	ed, ing, er, s
		brewery	ies
br		bribe	d, ∉ing, ry, s
brace	d, ∉ing, s	brick	ed, ing, laying, layer, work, yard, s
bracelet	s	bridal* (of a bride, wedding)	-gown
bracken		bride	groom, smaid, s
bracket	ed, ing, s	bridge	d, ∉ing, head, s
brag	ged, ging, gart, s	bridle* (horse's headgear)	-path, road, s
braid	ed, ing, s	brief	ed, ing, er, est, ly, ness, case, s
brain	ed, ing, less, storm, wave, s	brigade	s
brainy	ier, iest, ily, iness	brigand	s

			∉ Drop e before adding *ing*
		boy	bread	bridal
*	born	bough	boulder	buoy	break	bred	bridle
	borne	bow	bolder		brake		

bu

bubble	d, ϵing - bath - gum, s
bubbly	ier, iest, iness
buccaneer	s
buck	ed, ing, skin, s
bucket	ful, s
buckle	d, ϵing, s
bud	ded, ding, s
budge	d, ϵing, s
budgerigar	s
budget	ed, ing, s
buffalo	es or **buffalo**
buffer	s
buffet	ed, ing, s
bugle	-call, r, s
build	ing, er, s
built	
bulb	s
bulge	d, ϵing, s

bright	er, est, ly, ness
brighten	ed, ing, s
brilliance	
brilliant	ly
brim	med, ming, ful, s
bring	ing, s
brink	s
brisk	er, est, ly, ness
bristle	d, ϵing, s
bristly	ier, iest, iness
brittle	ness
broad	er, est, ly, -minded, side, s
broaden	ed, ing, s
broadcast	ing, er, s
brocade	s
broccoli	
broke	
broken	-down, -hearted
bronchitis	

bronze	d, ₵ing, s
brood	es
brook	ed, ing, y, s
broom	s
broth	stick, s
brother	s
brother(s)-in-law	ly, s
brought (bring)	
brow	s
brown	ed, ing, er, est, ish, ness, s
brownie	s
bruise	d, ₵ing, r, s
brunette	s
brush	ed, ing, es
Brussels sprouts	
brutal	ity, ly
brute	s

bulk	
bulky	ier, iest, ily, iness
bull	dog, fight, frog, ring, -terrier; s
bull's-eye	s
bulldoze	d, ₵ing, r, s
bullet	-hole, -proof, -wound, s
bulletin	s
bullion	
bullock	s
bully	s
bullied	ing
	ies
bulrush	es
bumble-bee	s
bump	ed, ing, er, s
bumpy	ier, iest, ily, iness
bunch	ed, ing, es
bundle	d, ₵ing, s
bung	ed, ing, -hole, s

₵ Drop e before adding ing

by

by* (near to, etc.)	
bye* (a run)	
bygone	
by-pass	ed, ing, es
bystander	s
byway	s

ca

cabaret	s
cabbage	s
cabin	-boy, s
cabinet	-maker, s
cable	d, éing, gram, -car, s
cackle	d, éing, r, s
cactus	es or **cacti**
caddie* (golfer's club-carrier)	d, s
caddying	
caddy* (tea box)	ies

bungalow	s
bungle	d, éing, r, s
bunk	s
bunker	ed, ing, s
Bunsen burner	s
bunting	
buoy* (floating marker)	ant, ed, ing, s
burden	ed, ing, some, s
bureau	x or s
burglar	-alarm, s
burglary	ies
burgle	d, éing, s
burial	-ground, -place, s
burly	ier, iest, ily, iness
burn	ed, ing, er, s
burnt or **burned**	
burrow	ed, ing, er, s
burst	ing, s
bury* (cover)	ing

buried	ies
bus	man, men, es
busby	ies
bush	es
bushy	ier, iest, ily, iness
business	man, men, es
bustle	d, e̸ing, ness
busy	ing, ness
busied	ier, iest, ily, ies
butcher	ed, ing, s
butler	s
butter	ed, ing, scotch, cup, s
butterfly	ies
button	ed, ing, -hole, s
buy* (purchase)	ing, er, s
buzz	ed, ing, es
buzzer	s
buzzard	s

cadet	s
cadge	d, e̸ing, r, s
café	s
cafeteria	s
cage	d, e̸ing, s
cake	d, e̸ing, s
calamity	ies
calculate	d, e̸ing, s
calculation	s
calculator	s
calendar	s
calf	skin, **calves**
call	ed, ing, er, s
calm	ed, ing, er, est, ly, ness, s
camel	-hair, s
camera	man, men, s
camouflage	d, e̸ing, s

e̸ Drop e before adding ing

*	buoy	bury
	boy	beret
		berry

buy	caddie
bye	caddy
by	

camp ed, ing, er, -bed, -fire, site, s
campaign ed, ing, er, s
canal s
canary ies
cancel led, ling, lation, s
candidate s
candle -light, wick, stick, s
candy ied, ies
cane d, ∉ing, s
cannibal ism, s
cannon ed, -ball, -shot, s or **cannon**
cannot
can't (cannot)
canoe d, ing, ist, s
canteen s
canter ed, ing, s
canvas* (strong cloth) es
canvass* (seek votes, orders) ed, ing, es
canyon s

career ed, ing, s
caress ed, ing, es
cargo es
caricature d, ∉ing, s
carnation s
carnival s
carnivorous
carol led, ling, ler, -singer, s
carpenter s
carpentry
carpet ed, ing, -sweeper, s
carriage way, s
carrot s
carry ing
carried ies
carrier -bag, -pigeon, s
cart ed, ing, -load, -horse, -wheel, s
carton s
cartoon ed, ing, ist, s

capable	y	cartridge	-belt, -case, s
cape	s	carve	d, e̸ing, r, s
capital	s	cascade	d, e̸ing, s
capsize	d, e̸ing, s	case	s
capsule	s	cash	ed, ing, -box, es
captain	ed, ing, s	cashier	s
captive	s	cask	s
captivity	ies	casket	s
capture	d, e̸ing, s	casserole	s
car	-load, -park, port, s	cassette	-player, -recorder, s
caramel	s	cast	ing, s
caravan	ned, ning, ner, s	castaway	s
carcasses or carcase	s	castle	s
card	board, -game, -room, -table, s	castor oil	
cardigan	s	casual	ly, ness, s
care	d, e̸ing free, taker, s	casualty	ies
careful	ly, ness	catalogue	d, e̸ing, s
careless	ly, ness	catapult	ed, ing, s

e̸ Drop e before adding ing

canvas
* canvass

ce

catastrophe	s
catch	ier, iest, iness
catchy	ed, ing, er, s
cater	s
caterpillar	s
cathedral	s
Catherine wheel	s
Catholic	s
catkin	s
cattle	-market, -shed, -show, -truck
caught	
cauldron	s
cauliflower	s
cause	d, ∉ing, s
caution	ed, ing, s
cautious	ly, ness
cavalier	s
cavalry	
cave	d, ∉ing, -man, -men, -dweller, s

cha

cemetery	ies
cent* (coin)	s
centigrade	
centimetre	s
central	ly
centre	d, ∉ing, -forward, -piece, s
century	ies
cereal* (wheat, oats, etc.)	s
ceremony	ies
certain	ly, ty
certificate	s

ch

chaffinch	es
chain	ed, ing, -mail, -saw, -store, s
chair	ed, ing, man, woman, -lift, s
chalet	s
chalk	ed, ing, s

cavern		s
cavity		ies

ce

cease		d, éing, less, lessly, s
cedar		s
ceiling* (roof of room)		s
celandine		s
celebrate		d, éing, s
celebration		s
celebrity		ies
celery		
cell* (small room)		s
cellar** (underground room)		s
cello		s
cellophane		
cement		ed, ing, -mixer, s

ceiling	cell	cellar
sealing	sell	seller
*		

chalky		ier, iest, iness
challenge		d, éing, r, s
chamber		maid, s
chamois		-leather
champagne		s
champion		ed, ing, ship, s
chance		d, éing, s
chandelier		s
change		able, d, éing, s
channel		led, ling, s
chant		ed, ing, s
chaos		
chaotic		ally
chapel		s
chapter		s
char		red, ring, woman, women, s
character		istic, s
charade		s

é Drop e before adding ing

cent	cereal
sent	serial
scent	

charcoal	d, ɖing, r, s	chick	weed, s
charge	eer, s	chicken	-feed, -wire, s or **chicken**
chariot	ies	chicken-pox	
charity		chief	ly, tain, s
charm	ed, ing, er, s	chilblain	s
chart	ed, ing, -room, s	child	ish, hood, like, less, **children**
charter	ed, ɖing, s	chill	ed, ing, er, s
chase	d, ɖing, r, s	chilly	ier, iest, ily, iness
chasm	s	chime	d, ɖing, s
chat	ted, ting, s	chimney	-pot, -stack, -sweep, s
chatter	ed, ing, er, s	chimpanzee	s
chatty	ier, iest, ily, iness	chin	-strap, s
chauffeur	s	china	-shop, ware
cheap	er, est, ly, ness	chink	ed, ing, s
cheapen	ed, ing, s	chintz	es
cheat	ed, ing, er, s	chip	ped, ping, per, s
check*	ed, ing, er, -list, -out, -point, s	chirp	ed, ing, s
check* (pattern)	ed, s	chirpy	ier, iest, ily, iness
cheek	ed, ing, -bone, s	chisel	led, ling, s

cheeky ier, iest, ily, iness, s	**chivalrous** ly
cheer ed, ing, -leader, s	**chivalry**
cheerful ly, ness	**chlorine**
cheerless ly, ness	**chloroform** ed, ing, s
cheery ier, iest, ily, iness	**chocolate** s
cheese burger, cake, cloth, -straw, s	**choice** r, st, ly, ness, s
chef s	**choir*** (of singers) -boy, -master, s
chemical ly, s	**choke** d, ƈing, s
chemist s	**choose** ƈing, s
chemistry	**chose** n
cheque* (money-order) -book, s	**chop** ped, ping, per, s
cherish ed, ing, es	**chopstick** s
cherry ies	**chorus** ed, ing, es
chess -board, -piece, -man, -men	**chow** ed, ing, s
chest s	**christen** ed, ing, s
chestnut -tree, s	**Christ**
chew ed, ing, y, er; s	**Christian** ity, s
chewing-gum	**Christmas** -box, es, -time, -tree, sy

ƈ Drop e before adding ing

* check
  cheque

* choir
  quire

chromium	-plated, -plating
chrysalis	es
chrysanthemum	s
chubby	ier, iest, ily, iness
chuckle	d, ∂ing, s
chug	ged, ging, s
chum	med, ming, s
chummy	ier, iest, ily, iness
chunk	s
church	es
churchyard	s
churn	ed, ing, s
chute* (a slide)	s
chutney	s

ci

cider or **cyder**	s
cigar	-case, -holder, -lighter; s

cl

claim	ed, ing, s
clamber	ed, ing, s
clammy	ier, iest, ily, iness
clamp	ed, ing, s
clang	ed, ing, s
clank	ed, ing, s
clap	ped, ping, per; s
clash	ed, ing, es
clasp	ed, ing, s
class	ed, ing, es, rooms
classic	al, s
clatter	ed, ing, s
claw	ed, ing, s
clay	ey, -pigeon, -pipe, -pit, s
clean	ed, ing, er, est, ly, ness, s
cleanliness	
cleanse	d, ∂ing, r; s
clear	ed, ing, er, est, ly, ness, s

cigarette	-case, -holder, -lighter; s
cinder	-path, -track; s
cine-	camera, film, projector
cinema	-goer; s
circle	d, e̸ing, s
circular	s
circulate	d, e̸ing, s
circulation	s
circumference	s
circumstance	s
circus	es
cistern	s
citizen	es
city	ies
civil	ity, ly
civilian	s
civilization	s
civilize	d, e̸ing, s

chute
shoot
*

clench	ed, ing, es
clergy	man, men
clerk	s
clever	er, est, ly, ness
click	ed, ing, s
client	s
cliff	s
climate	-top, s
climb	ed, ing, er; s
cling	ing, s
clinic	al, ally, s
clink	ed, ing, er; s
clip	ped, ping, per; s
cloak	ed, ing, room, s
clock	ed, ing, wise, work, -tower; s
cloister	ed, ing, s
close (shut)	d, e̸ing, s
close (near; stuffy)	r, st, ly, ness

e̸ Drop e before adding ing

cloth s
clothe d, éing, s
clothes -basket, -horse, -line, -peg
cloud ed, ing, less, lessly, burst, s
cloudy ier, iest, ily, iness
clover s
clown ed, ing, s
club bed, bing, house, room, s
cluck ed, ing, s
clue less, s
clump ed, ing, s
clumsy ier, iest, ily, iness
clung
cluster ed, ing, s
clutch ed, ing, es
clutter ed, ing, s

cocoon s
code d, éing, s
coffee -bar, -bean, -cup, -pot, -table, s
coffin s
coil ed, ing, s
coin age, ed, ing, s
coincide d, éing, s
coincidence s
cold er, est, ish, ly, ness, -storage, s
collapse d, éing, s
collapsible
collar -bone, -stud, s
collect ed, ing, ion, or, s
college s
collide d, éing, s
collision s
collie s
collier s
colliery ies
colonel* (officer) s

co	
coach	man, men, ed, ing, es
coal	man, men, -mine, -miner, s
coarse* (rough)	r, st, ly, ness
coast	al, ed, ing, line, guard, s
coat	ed, ing, -hanger, s
coax	es
cobble	d, éing, r, -stone, s
cobra	s
cobweb	by, s
cock	ed, ing, -fight, pit, tail, s
cockatoo	s
cockerel	s
cockle	-shell, s
cockney	s
cockroach	es
cocoa	
coconut	-matting, -milk, -palm, s

* coarse
 course

colonize	d, éing, s
colony	ies
colossal	ly
colour	ed, ing, ful, less, -scheme, s
column	s
comb	ed, ing, s
combat	ed, ing, s
combination	s
combine	d, éing, -harvester, s
come	éing, s
comedian (masc.)	
comedienne (fem.)	s
comedy	ies
comet	s
comfort	able, ably, ed, ing, s
comic	al, ally, s
command	ed, ing, er, ment, s
commemorate	d, éing, s

é Drop e before adding ing

colonel
kernel

commence	d, ¢ing, ment, s
comment	ed, ing, ator, s
commentary	ies
commerce	
commercial	s
commission	ed, ing, aire, er, s
commit	ted, ting, ment, s
committee	-room, s
common	er, est, ly, ness, -room, s
commotion	s
communicate	d, ¢ing, s
communication	s
communion	
community	ies
compact	s
companion	ship, s
company	ies
comparative	ly, s
compare	d, ¢ing, s

conceal	ed, ing, ment, s
conceit	ed, edly
concentrate	d, ¢ing, s
concentration	
concern	ed, ing, s
concert	s
conclude	d, ¢ing, s
conclusion	s
concrete	d, ¢ing, s
condemn	ed, ing, ation, s
condition	ed, ing, er, s
conduct	ed, ing, or, s
conductress	es
conference	s
confess	ed, ing, es
confession	s
confetti	
confide	d, ¢ing, s
confidence	

comparison	s	confident	ial, ially, ly
compartment	s	confirm	ed, ing, ation, s
compass	es	confiscate	d, e̶ing, s
compel	led, ling, s	confuse	d, e̶ing, s
compete	d, e̶ing, s	confusion	s
competition	s	congratulate	d, e̶ing, s
competitor	s	congratulation	s
complain	ed, ing, s	congregate	d, e̶ing, s
complaint	s	congregation	s
complete	d, e̶ing, ly, ness, s	conjure	d, e̶ing, s
complexion	s	conjurer or conjuror	s
complicate	d, e̶ing, s	conker* (horse-chestnut)	s
compliment	ed, ing, ary, s	connect	ed, ing, ion, s
compose	d, e̶ing, r, s	conquer* (defeat)	ed, ing, or, s
composition	s	conquest	s
comprehensive school		conscience	s
computer	s	conscientious	ly, ness
comrade	ship, s	conscious	ly, ness

e̶ Drop **e** before adding **ing**

* conker
* conquer

cook	ed, ing, er, ery, book, house, s
cool	ed, ing, er, est, ish, ly, ness, s
co-operate	d, ɇing, s
co-operation	
copper	s
coppice or **copse**	
copy	ing
copied	ies
coral	-island, -reef, s
cord	s
cordial	s
cordon	ed, ing, s
corduroy	s
core* (middle of apple, etc.)	d, ɇing, s
corgi	s
cork	ed, ing, screw, s
corn	-cob, field, flake, s
corned beef	
corner	ed, ing, s

consent	ed, ing, s
consequence	s
consequent	ly
conservative	s
consider	ed, ing, able, ably, ate, ation, s
consist	ed, ing, s
consolation	-prize, s
conspicuous	ly, ness
constable	s
constant	ly
construct	ed, ing, ion, or, s
consult	ed, ing, ation, s
consume	d, ɇing, r, s
contact	ed, ing, s
contain	ed, ing, er, s
contemporary	ies
content	ed, ing, ment, s
contest	ed, ing, ant, s
continent	al, s

continual		cornet	s
continue	d, €ing, s	coronation	s
continuation		corporal	s
continuous	ly, ness	corporation	s
contradict	ed, ing, ion, s	corps* (group of cadets, etc.)	**corps**
contribute	d, €ing, s	corpse	s
contribution	s	correct	ed, ing, ion, ly, ness, s
control	led, ling, ler, -column, -lever, s	correspond	ed, ing, ence, ent, s
convalesce	d, €ing, nt, s	corridor	s
convenience	s	cosmetic	s
convenient	ly	cosmonaut	s
convent	s	cost	ing, s
conversation	s	costly	ier, iest, iness
convert	ed, ing, s	coster	monger, s
convey	ed, ing, ance, s	costume	s
convict	ed, ing, ion, s	cosy	ier, iest, ily, iness, ies
convince	d, €ing, s	cottage	s
convoy	ed, ing, s	cotton	wool, s

€ Drop **e** before adding ing

* core
   corps

couch	es
cough	ed, ing, er; -drop, -mixture, s
could	
couldn't (could not)	
council	lor, -chamber, -house, s
count	ed, ing, er; less, -down, s
counter	ed, ing, -attack, foil, s
countess	es
country	ies
county	ies
couple	d, ɇing, s
coupon	s
courage	
courageous	ly, ness
course* (track; direction; of course)	s
court	ed, ing, ier, room, ship, yard, s
courtesy	ies
cousin	ly, s
cove	s

crank	ed, ing, s
crash	ed, ing, es
crate	d, ɇing, ful, s
crater	s
crave	d, ɇing, s
crawl	ed, ing, er, s
crayon	ed, ing, s
craze	d, ɇing, s
crazy	ier, iest, ily, iness
creak* (noise)	ed, ing, s
creaky	ier, iest, ily, iness
cream	ed, ing, er; -cake, -cheese, s
creamy	ier, iest, ily, iness
crease	d, ɇing, s
create	d, ɇing, s
creature	s
credit	able, ed, ing, or, s
creek* (small bay, sea-coast inlet)	s
creep	ing, er, s

cover ed, ing, s	**creepy** ier, iest, ily, iness
cow boy, hand, herd, hide, shed, s	**cremate** d, éing, s
coward s	**crematorium** s
cowardice	**creosote** d, éing, s
cowardly iness	**crept**
cowslip s	**crescent** s
	crest ed, ing, fallen, s
cr	**crevice** s
	crew ed, ing, s
crab -apple, -pot, s	**crib** bed, bing, ber, s
crack ed, ing, er, s	**cricket** ing, er, -field, s
crackle d, éing, s	**cried**
cradle d, éing, s	**crier** s
craft sman, smen, s	**cries**
crafty ier, iest, ily, iness	**crime** s
cram med, ming, mer, s	**criminal** s
cramp ed, ing, s	**crimson** s
crane d, éing, -driver; s	**cringe** d, éing, s

é Drop e before adding ing

* course   creak
    coarse   creek

cro cru

crinkle	d, éing, s
crinkly	ier, iest, iness
cripple	d, éing, s
crisp	ed, ing, er, est, ly, ness, s
crispy	ier, iest, ily, iness
critic	al, ally, ism, s
criticize	d, éing, s
croak	ed, ing, er, s
croaky	ier, iest, ily, iness
crochet	ed, ing, -hook, s
crockery	
crocodile	s
crocus	es
crook	s
crooked	ly, ness
crop	ped, ping, per, s
croquet	
cross	ed, ing, er, est, ly, ness, es
crossroad	s

cry cu

crumple	d, éing, s
crunch	ed, ing, es
crusade	d, éing, r, s
crush	ed, ing, es
crust	s
crusty	ier, iest, ily, iness
crutch	es
cry	ing
cried	ies
crypt	s
crystal	s

cu

Cub Scout	s
cube	d, éing, s
cubicle	s
cuckoo	-clock, s
cucumber	s

crossword	s
crouch	ed, ing, es
crow	ed, ing, bar, s
crowd	ed, ing, s
crown	ed, ing, s
crucify	ing
crucified	ies
crucifix	es
crucifixion	s
crude	r, st, ly, ness
cruel	ler, lest, ly
cruelty	ies
cruet	s
cruise	d, éing, r, s
crumb	s
crumble	d, éing, s
crumbly	ier, iest, iness
crumpet	s

cuddle	d, éing, some, s
cue* (hint; billiard-stick)	s
cuff	-link, s
cul-de-sac	**culs-de-sac**
culprit	s
cultivate	d, éing, s
cultivation	
cunning	ly
cup	ful, s
cupboard	s
curate	s
curator	s
curb* (hold back)	ed, ing, s
curdle	d, éing, s
cure	d, éing, s
curio	s
curiosity	ies
curious	ly, ness

é Drop e before adding ing

*	cue	curb
	queue	kerb

cy da

curl	ed, ing, er, s
curly	ier, iest, ily, iness
currant* (fruit)	-bread, -bun, -cake, s
current* (flow of water, air, etc.)	s
curry	ied, ies
curse	d, ₫ing, s
curt	ly, ness
curtain	ed, ing, s
curtsy	ing
curtsied	
curve	d, ₫ing, s
cushion	s
custard	-powder, -pie, s
custom	s
customer	s
cut	‑ting, ter, ‑price, ‑rate, ‑throat, s
cutlass	es
cutlery	

daft	er, est, ly, ness
dagger	s
dahlia	s
daily	ies
dainty	ier, iest, ily, iness, ies
dairy	ies
daisy	ies
dale	s
Dalmatian	s
dam	med, ming, s
damage	d, ₫ing, s
dame	s
damp	ed, ing, er, est, ly, ness, s
dampen	ed, ing, er, s
damson	-tree, s
dance	d, ₫ing, r, -band, -floor, s
dandelion	s
danger	s
dangerous	ly

cy

cycle	d, éing, -clip, s
cyclist	s
cyclone	s
cygnet* (young swan)	s
cylinder	s
cymbal	ist, s
cypress	es

da

dab	bed, bing, ber, s
dabble	d, éing, r, s
dachshund	s
dad	s
daddy	ies
daffodil	s

dangle	d, éing, s
dank	er, est, ly, ness
dapple	d, éing, -grey, s
dare	d, éing, -devil, s
dark	er, est, ly, ness
darken	ed, ing, s
darling	s
darn	ed, ing, er, s
dart	ed, ing, -board, s
dash	ed, ing, es
date	d, éing, -stamp, -palm, s
daub	ed, ing, er, s
daughter	s
dawdle	d, éing, r, s
dawn	ed, ing, s
day	break, dream, light, time, s
daze	d, éing, s
dazzle	d, éing, r, s

*	cygnet	currant
	signet	current

de

dead	-beat, -end, -heat, line, lock, ness
deaden	ed, ing, er, s
deadly	ier, iest, iness
deaf	-aid, er, est, ly, ness
deafen	ed, ing, s
deal	ing, er, s
dealt	
dear** (beloved; costly)	er, est, ly, ness, s
death	ly, -bed, -blow, -rate, -ray, -trap, s
debate	d, ∉ing, r, s
debris	
debt	or, s
decay	ed, ing, s
deceit	ful, fully, s
deceive	d, ∉ing, r, s
December	
decent	ly
decide	d, dly, ∉ing, s

de

defend	ed, ing, er, s
defiant	ly
definite	ly
degree	s
delay	ed, ing, s
deliberate	ly, ness, d, ∉ing, s
delicacy	ies
delicate	ly, ness
delicious	ly, ness
delight	ed, ing, s
delightful	ly, ness
deliver	ed, ing, ance, s
delivery	ies
deluge	d, ∉ing, s
demand	ed, ing, s
demolish	ed, ing, es
demon	s
demonstrate	d, ∉ing, s
demonstration	s

decimal	s		**demonstrator**	s
decipher	ed, ing, s		**dense**	r, st, ly, ness
decision	s		**dent**	ed, ing, s
deck	ed, ing, -chair, s		**dentist**	s
declare	d, éing, s		**deny**	ing
decline	d, éing, s		**denied**	ies
decorate	d, éing, s		**depart**	ed, ing, ure, s
decoration	s		**department**	s
decorator	s		**depend**	ed, ing, able, ent, s
decrease	d, éing, s		**deport**	ed, ing, ation, s
deduct	ed, ing, ion, s		**deposit**	ed, ing, or, s
deed	s		**depot**	s
deep	er, est, ly, ness		**depth**	-charge, s
deepen	ed, ing, s		**deputy**	ies
deer* (animal)	skin, stalker, -park, **deer**		**derail**	ed, ing, ment, s
defeat	ed, ing, s		**derelict**	s
defect	ive, s		**descant**	-recorder, s
defence	less, lessly, s		**descend**	ed, ing, ant, s

é Drop **e** before adding **ing**

*   dear
    deer

di

diagram	s
dial	led, ling, ler, s
dialect	s
dialogue	s
diameter	s
diamond	s
diary	ies
dictate	d, ∉ing, s
dictation	s
dictionary	ies
didn't (did not)	
die* (small spotted cube)	**dice**
die* (lose life)	s
died* (lost life)	
dying* (losing life)	
diet	ed, ing, ician, s
differ	ed, ing, ence, s
different	ly

descent	s
describe	d, ∉ing, s
description	s
desert (sandy place)	s
desert* (run away)	ed, ing, ion, er, s
deserve	d, ∉ing, s
design	ed, ing, er, s
desire	d, ∉ing, s
desk	s
desolate	d, ∉ing, ly, ness, s
despair	ed, ing, ingly, s
despatch or **dispatch**	ed, ing, es
desperate	ly, ness
desperation	
despise	d, ∉ing, s
despite	
dessert* (fruit, pudding, etc.)	-spoon, s
destination	s
destroy	ed, ing, er, s

destruction		**difficult**	
destructive	ly, ness	**difficulty**	difficulties
detach	ed, ing, es	**dig**	ging, ger, s
detail	ed, ing, s	**digest**	ed, ing, ion, ive, s
detain	ed, ing, s	**dignify**	ied, ies
detect	ed, ing, ion, or, s	**dignity**	
detective	s	**dike** or **dyke**	s
detention	s	**dilapidated**	
determination		**dilute**	d, ting, s
determine	d, ting, s	**dim**	med, ming, mer, mest, ly, ness, s
detest	able, ed, ing, s	**dimension**	s
develop	ed, ing, er, ment, s	**dimple**	d, ting, s
device	s	**dine**	d, ting, r, s
devil	ish, ry, ment, s	**dining**	-car, -hall, -room, -table
devise	d, ting, s	**dinghy**	ies
devour	ed, ing, er, s	**dingy**	ier, iest, ily, iness
dew* (moisture)	y, -drop, -fall, -pond, s	**dinner**	-hour, -service, -table, -time, s
		dinosaur	

é Drop e before adding ing

desert	dew	die	dying	
dessert	due	dye	dyeing	
*	Jew		died	dyed

dip	ped, ping, per, s
diploma	s
direct	ed, ing, ly, ness, ive, or, s
directory	ies
dirt	-track
dirtied	ier, iest, ily, iness, ies
dirty	ing
disable	d, éing, ment, s
disadvantage	s
disagree	able, d, ing, ment, s
disappear	ed, ing, ance, s
disappoint	ed, ing, ment, s
disarm	ed, ing, ament, s
disarrange	d, éing, ment, s
disaster	s
disastrous	ly
disc or **disk**	s
discharge	d, éing, s

dismal	ly, ness
dismantle	d, éing, s
dismay	ed, ing, s
dismiss	ed, ing, es
dismount	ed, ing, s
disobedience	
disobedient	ly
disobey	ed, ing, s
disorder	ly, s
dispatch or **despatch**	ed, ing, es
dispensary	ies
dispense	d, éing, r, s
display	ed, ing, s
displease	d, éing, s
dispute	d, éing, s
disqualify	ing
disqualified	ies, ication
dissatisfy	ing
dissatisfied	ies, action

disciple	s	**dissolve**	d, ¢ing, s
discipline	d, ¢ing, s	**distance**	s
discontent	ed, edly, ment, s	**distant**	ly
discothèque or **disco**	-club, -dancing, s	**distinct**	ion, ive, ly, ness
discourage	d, ¢ing, ment, s	**distinguish**	able, ed, ing, es
discover	ed, ing, er, s	**distract**	ed, ing, ion, s
discovery	ies	**distress**	ed, ing, es
discuss	ed, ing, es	**distribute**	d, ¢ing, s
discussion	s	**district**	s
disease	ed, ing, es	**disturb**	ed, ing, ance, s
disgrace	d, ¢ing, s	**ditch**	ed, ing, es
disgraceful	ly, ness	**divan**	s
disguise	d, ¢ing, s	**dive**	d, ¢ing, r, s
disgust	ed, ing, s	**divert**	ed, ing, s
dish	ed, ing, es	**divide**	d, ¢ing, r, s
dishearten	ed, ing, s	**division**	s
dishonest	ly, y	**divorce**	d, ¢ing, e, s
dislike	able, d, ¢ing, s	**dizzy**	ier, iest, ily, iness

¢ Drop **e** before adding **ing**

do

docile	ly
dock	ed, ing, er, yard, s
doctor	s
document	ed, ing, s
dodge	d, ꬲing, r, s
doe* (female animal)	
does	
doesn't (does not)	
doing	
dole	d, ꬲing, ful, fully, s
doll	s
dollar	s
dolphin	s
domestic	ally, s
domesticate	d, ꬲing, s
domino	es
donate	d, ꬲing, s
donation	s

dr

drab	ber; best, ly, ness
drag	ged, ging, -net, s
dragon	s
dragonfly	ies
drain	age, ed, ing, -pipe, s
drake	s
drama	tic, tist, s
dramatize	d, ꬲing, s
drank	
drape	d, ꬲing, s
draper	s
drapery	ies
drastic	ally
draught	sman, smen, -board, s
draughty	ier; iest, ily, iness
draw	n, ing, er, s
drawbridge	s
drawer	s

done	
donkey	s
don't (do not)	
doom	ed, ing, sday, s
door	bell, keeper, mat, step, way, s
dormitory	ies
dose	d, €ing, s
dot	ted, ting, s
double	d, €ing, -jointed, -decker, s
doubt	ed, ing, less, er, s
doubtful	ly, ness
dough* (moist flour)	
douse or dowse	d, €ing, s
dove	cote, s
dowdy	ier, iest, ily, iness
down	stairs, hill, fall, pour, ward, s
doze	d, €ing, s
dozen	s or dozen

drawing	-board, -paper, -pin, -room, s
dread	ed, ing, s
dreadful	ly, ness
dream	ed, ing, land, like, s
dreamt or dreamed	
dreamy	ier, iest, ily, iness
dreary	ier, iest, ily, iness
dredge	d, €ing, r, s
drench	ed, ing, es
dress	ed, ing, es
dresser	s
dressing	-gown, -case, -room, -table, s
dressmaker	s
drew	
dribble	d, €ing, r, s
drift	ed, ing, er, s
drill	ed, ing, er, s
drink	able, ing, er, s

€ Drop e before adding ing

*   doe
    dough

du

drip	ped, ping, s
drive	ɇing, r, way; s
driven	
drivel	led, ling, ler; s
drizzle	d, ɇing, s
drizzly	ier, iest, iness
dromedary	ies
drone	d, ɇing, s
droop	ed, ing, s
drop	ped, ping, per, let; s
drought	s
drove	
drown	ed, ing, s
drowse	d, ɇing, s
drowsy	ier, iest, ily, iness
drudgery	
drug	ged, ging, gist, -addict, store, s
drum	med, ming, mer, -major, stick, s
drunk	ard, s

dw dy

duly	
dumb	er, est, ly, ness
dummy	ies
dump	ed, ing, s
dumpling	s
dunce	s
dungarees	
dungeon	s
duplicate	d, ɇing, s
durable	ness
duration	
during	
dusk	
dusky	ier, iest, ily, iness
dust	ed, ing, man, men, bin, pan, er; s
dusty	ier, iest, ily, iness
dutiful	ly, ness
duty	ies

drunken	ly, ness
dry	ing, ness
dried	
dryer or **drier** (noun)	ier; iest, ies
dryly or **drily**	s

du

dual* (two; double)	
duchess	es
duck	ed, ing, ling, s
due* (expected; owing)	s
duel* (fight)	led, ling, list, s
duet	s
duffel or **duffle**	-bag, -coat, s
dug	-out
duke	dom, s
dull	ed, ing, er, est, ish, y, ness, s

due	dual
dew	duel
Jew	jewel
*	

dw

dwarf	ed, ing, s or **dwarves**
dwell	ed, ing, er, s
dwelling	-house, -place, s
dwelt or **dwelled**	
dwindle	d, éing, s

dy

dye* (colour)	r, s
dyed* (coloured)	
dyeing* (colouring)	
dying* (losing life)	
dyke or **dike**	s
dynamic	al, ally, s
dynamite	d, éing, s
dynamo	s

é Drop e before adding ing		
dye	dyed	dyeing
die	died	dying

ea

each	
eager	ly, ness
eagle	t, s
ear	ache, -drum, phone, -plug, -ring, s
earwig	s
earl	dom, s
early	ier, iest, iness
earn* (be paid)	ed, ing, er, s
earnt *or* earned	
earnest	ly, ness
earth	quake, worm, work, s
earthen	ware
ease	d, ∂ing, s
easy	ier, iest, ily, iness
easel	s
east	em, erly, ward, wards
Easter	-egg, s

ee ef eg ei el

edit	ed, ing, s
edition	ial, s
editor	
educate	d, ∂ing, s
education	al, ally, alist, ist

ee

eel	s
eerie *or* eery	ier, iest, ily, iness

ef

effect	ed, ing, s
effective	ly, ness
efficiency	
efficient	ly
effigy	ies
effort	less, lessly, s

eat	able, en, ing, er, s
eavesdrop	ped, ping, per, s

ec

eccentric	s
echo	ed, ing, es
éclair	s
eclipse	d, éing, s
economic	al, ally, s
economize	d, éing, s
economy	ies

ed

eddy	ing
eddied	ies
edge	d, éing, ways, wise, s
edible	ed, ing, ion, or, s

* earn
um

eg

egg	-cup, -shell, -spoon, -timer; s

ei

eiderdown	
either	

el

elaborate	d, éing, ly, ness, s
elapse	d, éing, s
elastic	ally, ity
elbow	ed, ing, s
elder	
eldest	
elect	ed, ing, ion, or, s

é Drop e before adding ing

em

electric	al, ally, s
electrician	s
electricity	
electrocute	d, ⁄ing, s
elegant	ly
elephant	s
elevator	s
elf	in, ish, **elves**
eligible	
eliminate	d, ⁄ing, s
elimination	
Elizabethan	s
elm	-tree, s
elocution	ist
elope	d, ⁄ing, ment, s
else	where

en

emptied	ier, iest, ily, iness, ies

en

enable	d, ⁄ing, s
enamel	led, ling, s
encamp	ed, ing, ment, s
enchant	ed, ing, ment, s
encircle	d, ⁄ing, s
enclose	d, ⁄ing, s
enclosure	s
encore	d, ⁄ing, s
encounter	ed, ing, s
encourage	d, ⁄ing, ment, s
encyclop(a)edia	s
end	ed, ing, less, lessly, s
endanger	ed, ing, s
endeavour	ed, ing, s
endure	d, ⁄ing, s
endurance	s

em			
embankment	s	**enemy**	ies
embark	ed, ing, ation, s	**energetic**	ally
embarrass	ed, ing, es	**energy**	ies
embarrassment	s	**enforce**	d, e̸ing, ment, s
emblem	s	**engage**	d, e̸ing, ment, s
embrace	d, e̸ing, s	**engine**	-driver, -room, s
embroider	ed, ing, s	**engineer**	ed, ing, s
embroidery	ies	**engrave**	d, e̸ing, r, s
emerald	s	**engulf**	ed, ing, s
emerge	d, e̸ing, s	**enjoy**	ed, ing, s
emergency	ies	**enlarge**	able, ed, ing, ment, s
emigrate	d, e̸ing, s	**enlist**	d, e̸ing, r, ment, s
emperor	s	**enormous**	ly, ness
empire	s	**enough**	
employ	ed, ing, ment, ee, er, s	**enquire** or **inquire**	d, e̸ing, r, s
empress	es	**enquiry** or **inquiry**	ies
empty	ing	**enrage**	d, e̸ing, s
		enrol	led, ling, ment, s

e̸ Drop **e** before adding **ing**

ep eq er   es ev

entangle	d, ding, ment, s
enter	ed, ing, s
enterprise	s
entertain	ed, ing, ment, er; s
enthusiasm	s
enthusiastic	ally
entire	ly, ness
entitle	d, ding, ment, s
entrance	s
entry	ies
envelope	s
envious	ly, ness
environment	al, alist, s
envy	ing
envied	ies

ep

epidemic	s
epilogue	s
episode	s

es

escalator	s
escapade	s
escape	d, ding, r, s
escort	ed, ing, s
Eskimo	s or es or **Eskimo**
especial	ly
espionage	s
esplanade	s
essay	ist, s
essence	s
essential	ly, s
establish	ed, ing, es
establishment	s
estate	s
estimate	d, ding, s
estuary	ies

eq

equal	led, ling, ly, s
equalize	d, éing, r, s
equator	ial
equip	ped, ping, ment, s
equivalent	ly

er

erase	d, éing, r, s
erect	ed, ing, ion, s
err	ed, ing, ant, s
errand	s
erratic	ally
error	s
erupt	ed, ing, ion, s

ev

evacuate	d, éing, s
evacuation	s
evade	d, éing, s
evaporate	d, éing, s
eve	s
even	ed, ing, ly, ness, s
evening	s
event	ful, less, s
eventual	ly
ever	green, lasting, more
every	body, one, thing, where
evict	ed, ing, ion, s
evidence	s
evident	ly
evil	ly, ness, s
evolve	d, éing, s
evolution	s

é Drop e before adding *ing*

ex

exact	ly, ness
exaggerate	d, ẻing, s
examination	s
examine	d, ẻing, r, s
examiner	s
example	s
exasperate	d, ẻing, s
excavate	d, ẻing, s
excavation	s
exceed	ed, ing, ingly, s
excel	led, ling, s
excellent	ly
except* (leaving out)	ed, ing, s
exception	al, ally, s
excess	ive, ively, es
exchange	d, ẻing, able, s
excitable	
excite	d, dly, ẻing, ment, s

ex

expect	ed, ing, ant, ation, s
expedition	s
expel	led, ling, s
expense	s
expensive	ly, ness
experience	d, ẻing, s
experiment	ed, ing, al, ally, s
expert	ise, ly, ness, s
expire	d, ẻing, s
explain	ed, ing, s
explanation	s
explode	d, ẻing, s
exploit	s
exploration	s
explore	d, ẻing, r, s
explosion	s
explosive	s
export	ed, ing, er, s
expose	d, ẻing, s

exclaim	ed, ing, s	exposure	s
exclude	d, éing, s	express	ed, ing, es
exclusive	ly, ness	expression	s
excursion	s	exquisite	ly, ness
excuse	d, éing, s	extend	ed, ing, s
execute	d, éing, s	extension	s
execution	er; s	extensive	ly, ness
exercise	d, éing, s	extent	s
exert	ed, ing, ion, s	exterior	
exhaust	ed, ing, ion, ible, ive, -pipe, s	extinct	ion
exhibit	ed, ing, or, s	extinguish	ed, ing, es
exhibition	s	extra	s
exile	d, éing, s	extract	ed, ing, ion, s
exist	ed, ing, ence, ent, s	extraordinary	ily, iness
exit	s	extravagance	s
expand	ed, ing, s	extravagant	ly
expanse	s	extreme	ly, s
expansion	s	extricate	d, éing, s

é Drop e before adding ing

* except
accept

ey fa

ey

eye d, ball, brow, lid, sight, sore, s
eyeing or **eying**
eyelash es

fa

fable s
fabulous ly, ness
face d, ding, -cloth, -flannel, s
fact s
factory ies
fade d, ding, s
faggot s
fail ed, ing, ure, s
faint er, est, ish, ly, ness, ed, s
fair* er, est, ish, ly, ness, ground, s
fairy ies
faith s

fe

farewell s
farm ed, ing, er, -house, yard, s
fascinate d, ding, s
fashion able, ably, ed, ing, s
fast er, est, ness, ed, ing, s
fasten ed, ing, er, s
fat ted, ter, test, ness, s
fatten ed, ing, s
fatty ier, iest, iness
fatal ly
fate* (destiny) d, ful, s
father* (parent) less, ly, s
fathom ed, ing, s
fatigue d, ding, s
fault ed, ing, less, lessly, s
faulty ier, iest, ily, iness
favour able, ably, ed, ing, itism, s
favourite s
fawn ed, ing, s

faithful	ly, ness
fake	d, ∉ing, s
falcon	er, ing, s
fall	en, ing, s
false	hood, r, st, ly, ness
falter	ed, ing, s
fame	d
familiar	ity, ly
family	ies
famine	s
famish	ed, ing, es
famous	ly
fan	ned, ning, ner, -belt, light, tail, s
fancy	ing
fancied	ier, iest, ies, iful, ifully
fantastic	ally
far	ther;* thest, -away, -off, -fetched
fare* (price of journey; food)	s

fe	
fear	ed, ing, some, s
fearful	ly, ness
fearless	ly, ness
feast	ed, ing, s
feat* (difficult deed)	s
feather	ed, ing, y, -bed, -duster, s
feature	d, ∉ing, s
February	s
fed	
fee	s
feeble	r, st, ness
feebly	
feed	ing, er; s
feel	ing, er; s
feet* (pl. of foot)	
feign	ed, ing, s
fell	ed, ing, s

∉ Drop e before adding ing

*	fair	farther	fate	feat
	fare	father	fête	feet

fi

fellow	ship, s
felt	
female	s
feminine	s
fence	d, *c*ing, r, s
fend	ed, ing, er; s
fern	s
ferocious	ly, ness
ferocity	
ferret	ed, ing, er; s
ferry	-boat, ing, man, men
ferried	ies
fertile	ly
fertilize	d, *c*ing, r, s
fester	ed, ing, s
festival	s
festive	ly
festivity	ies
fetch	ed, ing, es

fiend	ish, s
fierce	r, st, ly, ness
fiery	ier; iest, lily, iness
fight	ing, er; s
figure	d, *c*ing, s
file	d, *c*ing, s
fill	ed, ing, er; s
fillet	ed, ing, s
film	ed, ing, -set, -star, -studio, s
filter	ed, ing, -bed, -paper, -tip, s
filth	
filthy	ier; iest, lily, iness
final	ly, ist, s
finch	es
find* (found)	ing, er; s
fine	d,* *c*ing, s
fine	r, st, ly, ness
finger	ed, ing, -mark, -nail, -print, tip, s
finish	ed, ing, es

fête* (entertainment; festival)	d, éing, s
feud	s
feudal	ism
fever	ish, ishly, s
few	er, est

fi

fiancé* (masc.)	s
fiancée* (fem.)	s
fibre	glass, -tip, s
fiction	al
fictitious	
fiddle	d, éing, r, stick, s
fidget	ly, ness
field	ed, ing, sman, smen, er, s

fiord or **fjord**	s
fir*	-cone, -tree, s
fire	d, éing, man, men, place, work, s
fire	-alarm, -brigade, -engine, -escape, s
fire	-drill, -extinguisher, side, -station, s
firm	er, est, ly, ness, s
first	ly, -aid, -class, -floor, -hand, -rate, s
fish	ed, ing, -meal, -paste, y, es or **fish**
fisher	man, men, s
fishing	-boat, -line, -net, -rod, -tackle
fishmonger	s
fist	s
fit	ted, ting, ter, test, ful, ly, ness, ment, s
fix	ed, ing, es
fixture	s
fizz	ed, ing, es
fizzy	ier, iest, ily, iness
fizzle	d, éing, s

é Drop e before adding ing

	fir	fur
	find	fined
* fête		
fate		
fiancé		
fiancée		

fla fle fli

fl ged, ging, -day, -pole, -staff, s

flag	ged, ging, -day, -pole, -staff, s
flagon	s
flake	d, éing, s
flame	d, éing, -thrower, s
flamingo	es or s
flan	s
flank	ed, ing, s
flannel	s
flap	ped, ping, per, jack, s
flare	d, éing, s
flash	ed, ing, es
flashy	ier, iest, ily, iness
flask	s
flat	ter, test, ly, ness, let, s
flatten	ed, ing, s
flatter	ed, ing, y, er, s
flavour	ed, ing, less, s
flaw	ed, less, s

flo flu fly

flint	lock, stone, s
flinty	ier, iest, ily, iness
flip	ped, ping, per, s
flirt	ed, ing, ation, s
flit	ted, ting, s
float	ed, ing, er, s
flock	ed, ing, s
flog	ged, ging, s
flood	ed, ing, gate, lit, -lighting, -light, s
floor	ed, ing, -board, -cloth, -show, s
flop	ped, ping, s
floppy	ier, iest, ily, iness
floral	ly
florist	s
flounder	ed, ing, s
flour*	(ground wheat) ed, ing, y, s
flourish	ed, ing, es
flow	ed, ing, s
flower*	ed, ing, y, -bed, -garden, -pot, s

é Drop e before adding ing

flea* (insect)	-bite, -bitten, s	**flown**
fleck	ed, ing, s	**flu*** (influenza)
fledg(e)ling	s	**flue*** (chimney-pipe) -pipe, s
fled		**fluent** ly
flee* (run away)	ing, s	**fluff** ed, ing, s
fleece	d, éing, s	**fluffy** ier, iest, ily, iness
fleecy	ier, iest, ily, iness	**fluid** s
fleet	ing, er, est, ly, ness, s	**fluke** d, éing, s
flesh	-coloured, -wound	**flung**
flew* (fly)		**flurry** ing
flex	ible, ibility, ed, ing, es	**flurried**
flick	ed, ing, s	**flush** ed, ing, es
flicker	ed, ing, s	**fluster** ed, ing, s
flier or **flyer**	s	**flute** -player, s
flight	-deck, -recorder, -test, s	**flutter** ed, ing, s
flimsy	ier, iest, ily, iness	**fly** ies
flinch	ed, ing, es	**flyer** or **flier** s
fling	ing, s	**flying** -fish, -machine, -saucer, -squad

*	flea	flew	flour
	flee	flue	flower
		flu	

fo

foal ed, ing, s
foam ed, ing, -rubber, s
foamy ier, iest, iness
fo'c'sle or **forecastle** s
focus ed, ing, es or **foci**
foe s
fog ged, ging, -horn, -lamp, -signal, s
foggy ier, iest, ily, iness
foil ed, ing, s
fold ed, ing, er, s
foliage
folk -dance, lore, -song, -tale, s or **folk**
follow ed, ing, er, s
folly ies
fond er, est, ly, ness
fondle d, ding, s
food stuff, store, s
fool ed, ing, hardy, s

forever more
forfeit ed, ing, ure, s
forgave
forge d, ding, r, s
forgery ies
forget ting, -me-not, s
forgetful ly, ness
forgot ten
forgive n, ding, ness, s
fork ed, ing, s
forlorn ly, ness
form ed, ing, ation, s
former ly
formidable
formula e or s
fort* (castle)
forth* (forward) coming
fortification s
fortify ing

foolish	ly, ness
foot	ing, hold, path, sore, work, **feet**
football	er, s
footprint	s
footstep	s
for*	
forbad or forbade	
forbid	den, ding, s
force	d, ‡ing, s
ford	ed, ing, s
fore* (front)	arm, ground, most, man, men
forecast	ing, er, s
forehead	s
foreign	
foreigner	s
forest	ry, er, s
foretell	ing, er, s
foretold	

fortified	ies
fortnight	ly
fortress	es
fortunate	ly
fortune	-teller; s
forward	ed, ing, ly, ness, s
fossil	s
fought* (fight)	
foul* (dirty)	ed, ing, er, est, ly, ness, s
found	ed, ing, er
foundation	-stone, s
foundry	ies
fountain	-pen, s
fowl* (bird)	s or **fowl**
fox	es, hounds, hunting, y
foxglove	s
fox-terrier	s
foyer	s

‡ Drop e before adding ing

	for	fort	forth	foul
*	fore	fought	fourth (4th)	fowl
	four (4)			

fr

fr	
fraction	s
fracture	d, éing, s
fragile	ly, ness
fragment	s
fragrance	s
fragrant	ly
frail	er, est, ly, ty, ness
frame	d, éing, r, work, s
franc* (foreign coin)	s
frank* (candid, etc.)	er, est, ly, ness, s
frankincense	
frantic	ally, ly
fraud	s
fray	ed, ing, s
freak	ish, s
freckle	d, éing, s
free	d, ing, r, st, ly, dom, -style, -way, s
freeze* (ice; cold)	r, s

fu

fringe	d, éing, s
frisk	ed, ing, s
frisky	ier, iest, ily, iness
fritter	ed, ing, s
frivolous	ly, ness
frizz	ed, ing, es
frizzy	ier, iest, ily, iness
frock	s
frog	-spawn, s
frolic	ked, king, some, s
front	ed, ing, s
frontier	s
frost	ed, ing, -bite, -bitten, s
frosty	ier, iest, ily, iness
froth	ed, ing, s
frothy	ier, iest, ily, iness
frown	ed, ing, s
froze	n
frugal	ity, ly

		fruit	-cake, -juice, -tree, s
freezing	-point	fry	er; ing
freight	er; s	fried	ies
frequent	ly, ed, ing, s		
fresh	er, est, ly, ness	**fu**	
freshen	ed, ing, er; s		
fret	ted, ting, ful, fully, s	fudge	led, ling, s
fret	work, saw, s	fuel	led, ling, s
friar	s	fugitive	s
Friday	s	fulfil	led, ling, ment, s
fried	s	full	er, est, y, ness
friend	ship, s	fumble	d, éing, r; s
friendly	ier, iest, iness	fume	d, éing, s
frieze* (wall decoration)	s	fun	fair
frigate	s	funny	ier, iest, ily, iness
fright	s	function	ed, ing, s
frighten	ed, ing, s	fund	s
frightful	ly, ness	funeral	s
frill	ed, ing, y, s		

é Drop **e** before adding ing

| franc | freeze |
| frank | frieze |

*

ga

fungus	es or **fungi**
funnel	led, ling, s
fur* (animal's coat)	rier, s
furry	ier, iest, ily, iness
furious	ly, ness
furl	ed, ing, s
furnace	s
furnish	ed, ing, ings, es
furniture	
furrow	ed, ing, s
further	ed, ing, more, most, s
furthest	
furtive	ly, ness
fury	ies
furze	s
fuse	d, ding, s
fuselage	s
fuss	ed, ing, es
fussy	ier, iest, ily, iness

galleon	s
gallery	ies
galley	-slave, s
gallon	s
gallop	ed, ing, s
gallows	
gamble* (bet)	d, ding, r, s
gambol* (leap; frisk)	led, ling, s
game	r, st, ly, ness, keeper, s
gander	s
gang	ed, ing, ster, s
gangway	s
gaol or **jail**	ed, ing, er, s
gape	d, ding, r, s
garage	d, ding, s
garbage	
garden	ed, ing, er, s
gargle	d, ding, s
garland	ed, ing, s

futile	ly		**garlic**	
future	s		**garment**	s
fuzzy	ier, iest, ily, iness		**garret**	s
			garrison	ed, ing, s
	ga		**garter**	s
gabardine or **gaberdine**			**gas**	sed, sing, es
gabble	d, e̸ing, r, s		**gash**	ed, ing, es
gag	ged, ging, s		**gasp**	ed, ing, s
gaiety	ies		**gate*** (door)	keeper; post, way, s
gaily			**gather**	ed, ing, er, s
gain	ed, ing, s		**gaudy**	ier, iest, ily, iness
gait* (way of walking)			**gauge**	d, e̸ing, s
gala	s		**gauntlet**	s
galactic			**gauze**	s
galaxy	ies		**gave**	
gale	s		**gay**	er, est
gallant	ly, s		**gaily**	
			gaze	d, e̸ing, r, s

e̸ Drop **e** before adding **ing**

fur	gait
* fir	gate

ge

gear	ed, ing, case, -lever, wheel, s
geese	
Geiger counter	
gem	s
general	
generally	s
generate	d, éing, s
generation	s
generator	s
generosity	
generous	ly
genie	
genius	**genii** es
gentle	r, st, ness, man, men
gently	
genuine	ly, ness
geography	ical, ically
geologist	s

gi

giant	-killer; s
giddy	ier; iest; ily, iness
gift	ed, s
gigantic	ally
giggle	d, éing, r, s
gild* (cover with gold)	ed, ing, er; s
gilt* (gold covering)	
ginger	-ale, -beer, bread, -snap, s
gipsy or **gypsy**	ies
giraffe	s
girder	s
girl	s
Girl Guide	s
give	n, éing, r, s

gl

glacier	s
glad	der, dest, ly, ness

geology	ical, ically		gladden	ed, ing, s
geometry	ic, ical, ically		glade	s
Georgian			gladiator	s
geranium	s		gladiolus	es or **gladioli**
germ	s		glamour	
germinate	d, é(ing), s		glamorous	ly
germination			glance	d, é(ing), s
gesticulate	d, é(ing), s		glare	d, é(ing), s
gesture	d, é(ing), s		glass	es
get	ting, ter, away, s		gleam	ed, ing, s
geyser	s		glean	ed, ing, er, s
			glee	ful, fully
gh			glide	d, é(ing), r, s
ghastly	ier, iest, ily, iness		glimmer	ed, ing, s
gherkin	s		glimpse	d, é(ing), s
ghost	s		glint	ed, ing, s
ghostly	ier, iest, ily, iness		glisten	ed, ing, s
			glitter	ed, ing, s

*	gild	gilt
	guild	guilt

é Drop **e** before adding **ing**

gn go

gloat	ed, ing, s
globe	-trotter; s
glockenspiel	s
gloom	
gloomy	ier; iest, ily, iness
glory	ied, ies
glorious	ly
glossy	ier; iest, ily, iness
glove	-puppet, s
glow	ed, ing, -worm, s
glue	d, éing, y, -pot, s
glum	mer, mest, ly, ness

gn

gnash	ed, ing, es
gnat	-bite, s
gnaw	ed, ing, s
gnome	n, ed, ing, er, s

gondola	s
gondolier	s
gone	
gong	s
good	-hearted, ly, ness
good-bye	s
goose	**geese**
gooseberry	ies
gore	d, éing, s
gorge	d, éing, s
gorgeous	ly, ness
gorilla	s
gorse	s
gosling	s
gossip	ed, ing, er, s
govern	ed, ing, or, ment, s
governess	es
gown	s

goal	keeper, -kick, -mouth, -post, s
goat	herd, skin, s
gobble	d, éing, r, s
goblet	s
goblin	s
god	son, father, mother, parent, s
goddess	es
godchild	ren
goes	
going	s
goggle	d, éing, s
gold	en, -dust, -field, -mine, -smith
goldfish	es or **goldfish**
golf	ing, -club, -course, -links, er, s
golliwog	s

grab	bed, bing, ber, s
grace	d, éing, s
graceful	ly, ness
gracious	ly, ness
grade	d, éing, s
gradient	s
gradual	ly, ness
grain	s
grammar	
gramophone	s
grand	er, est, ly, ness, stand
grand	father, pa, mother, ma, parents
grandad or **grand-dad**	s
grandchild	ren
granny	ies

é Drop e before adding ing

gre gri

grange	s
granite	
grant	ed, ing, s
grape	fruit, -vine, s
graph	ed, ing, s
grapple	d, éing, s
grasp	ed, ing, s
grass	ed, ing, es
grassy	ier, iest, iness
grasshopper	s
grass-snake	s
grate* (fireplace; rub)	r,* d, éing, s
grateful	ly, ness
grating	s
gratitude	
grave	r, st, ly, ness
grave	-digger, stone, yard, s
gravel	led, ling, ly, -path, -pit, s
gravity	ies

gro gru

grill* (cook)	ed, ing, er, s
grille* (grating)	s
grim	mer, mest, ly, ness
grime	
grimy	ier, iest, ily, iness
grin	ned, ning, ner, s
grind	ing, er, stone, s
grip	ped, ping, per, s
gristle	
grit	ted, ting, ter, s
gritty	ier, iest, ily, iness
grizzle	d, éing, r, s
groan* (moan)	ed, ing, er, s
grocer	s
grocery	ies
groom	ed, ing, s
groove	d, éing, s
grope	d, éing, s
grotesque	ly, ness

gravy	ies	
graze	d, ∉ing, s	
grease	d, ∉ing, r, -paint, -proof, s	
greasy	ier, iest, ily, iness	
great* (large)	er;* est, ly, ness, s	
greed	ier, iest, ily, iness	
greedy	ier, iest, ly, ness, ery, ish, y, s	
green	s	
greengrocer	s	
greenhouse	s	
greet	ed, ing, s	
grenade	s	
grenadier	s	
grew		
grey	er, est, ly, ness, ish, hound, s	
grief	s	
grievance	s	
grieve	d, ∉ing, s	

grotto	es or s	
ground	ed, ing, sheet, sman, smen, s	
group	ed, ing, -leader; s	
grove	s	
grovel	led, ling, ler; s	
grow	th, ing, er; s	
grown* (got bigger)		
grown-up	s	
growl	ed, ing, er; s	
grub	bed, bing, ber; s	
grubby	ier, iest, ily, iness	
grudge	d, ∉ing, s	
gruel		
gruesome	ly, ness	
gruff	er, est, ly, ness	
grumble	d, ∉ing, r, s	
grumpy	ier, iest, ily, iness	
grunt	ed, ing, er; s	

∉ Drop e before adding ing

*	grate	grater	grill	groan
	great	greater	grille	grown

gu gy

guarantee	d, ing, s
guard	ed, ing, sman, smen, room, s
guardian	s
guess	ed,* ing, es, work
guest* (visitor)	-night, -house, -room, s
guide	d, éing, -dog, -book, -post, s
guild* (society)	hall, s
guillotine	d, éing, s
guilt* (wrongdoing)	less, lessly
guilty	ier, iest, ily, iness
guinea-pig	s
guitar	ist, s
gulf	s
gull	s
gully	ies
gulp	ed, ing, s
gum	med, ming, boil, -tree, s
gummy	ier, iest, iness

ha

habit	s
hack	ed, ing, er, s
haddock	s or **haddock**
hadn't (had not)	
hail	ed, ing, er, stone, storm, s
hair*	dresser, -dryer, pin, -slide, -style, s
hairy	ier, iest, iness
hake	s or **hake**
half	-price, -term, -time, -way, **halves**
halfpenny	ies or **halfpence**
hall* (room; passage)	way, s
hallo or **hello** or **hullo**	
halo	es or s
halt	ed, ing, s
halve	d, éing, s
hamburger	s
hammer	ed, ing, s
hammock	s

gun	ned, ning, ner, nery, man, men, s	
gun	fire, point, powder, shot, smith, s	
gurgle	d, €ing, s	
gush	ed, ing, s	
gust	ed, ing, s	
gusty	ier, iest, ily, iness	
gut	ted, ting, s	
gutter	s	
guy	s	
guzzle	d, €ing, r, s	
	gy	
gymkhana	s	
gymnasium	s or **gymnasia**	
gymnast	ic, s	
gymslip	s	
gypsy or **gipsy**	ies	

guild	guilt
gild	gilt

*	guessed
	guest

hamper	ed, ing, s
hamster	s
hand	ed, ing, bag, work, writing, ful, s
handcuff	ed, ing, s
handicap	ped, ping, per, s
handicraft	s
handiwork	
handkerchief	s
handle	d, €ing, r, -bar, s
handsome	r, st, ly, ness
handy	ier, iest, ily, iness
hang	ed, ing, -gliding, -glider, s
hangar* (aeroplane shed)	s
hanger** (for clothes, etc.)	s
happen	ed, ing, s
happy	ier, iest, ily, iness
harbour	ed, ing, -master, s
hard	er, est, ish, ly, ness, -hearted, ware

€ Drop **e** before adding **ing**

hair	
hare	
hall	hangar
haul	hanger

he

head	ed, ing, ache, long, light, way, s
headmaster	s
headmistress	es
headquarters	
heal* (cure)	ed, ing, er, s
health	
healthy	ier; iest, ily, iness
heap	ed, ing, s
hear* (listen)	ing, s
heard* (listened)	
heart* (of body)	ache, - broken, less, s
hearten	ed, ing, s
hearty	ier; iest, ily, iness
hearth	- rug, s
heat	ed, edly, ing, er, - stroke, wave, s
heath	land, s
heathen	s
heather	s

harden	ed, ing, er, s
hardship	s
hare* (animal)	s
hark	en
harm	ed, ing, s
harmful	ly, ness
harmless	ly, ness
harness	ed, ing, es
harp	ist, s
harpoon	ed, ing, - gun, s
harsh	er; est, ly, ness
hart* (stag)	s
harvest	ed, ing, er; s
hasn't (has not)	
haste	d, ding, s
hasten	ed, ing, s
hasty	ier; iest, ily, iness
hat	band, - peg, - pin, stand, - trick, ful, s
hatch	ed, ing, es

hatchet	s
hate	d, ∉ing, r, s
hateful	ly, ness
hatred	
haughty	ier, iest, ily, iness
haul* (pull)	age, ed, ing, er, s
haunt	ed, ing, s
have	∉ing
haven't (have not)	
haversack	s
havoc	
haw	thorn, s
hawk	ed, ing, er, s
hay	field, maker, making, rick, stack, s
hazard	ed, ing, ous, ously, s
hazel	nut, -tree, s
haze	s
hazy	ier, iest, ily, iness

heave	d, ∉ing, r, s
heaven	ly, ward, s
heavy	ier, iest, ily, iness
he'd (he had; he would)	
hedge	d, ∉ing, hog, row. - sparrow, s
heed	ed, ing, ful, less, s
heel* (back of foot)	ed, ing, s
hefty	ier, iest, ily, iness
heifer	s
height	s
heighten	ed, ing, s
heir* (one who inherits)	s
heiress	es
held	
helicopter	s
he'll (he will; he shall)	
hello or hallo or hullo	ed, ing, s
helm	sman, smen, s

∉ Drop e before adding ing

hare	hart	haul	heal	heal	hear	heard	heir
hair	heart	hall	heel	heel	here	herd	air

*

hi

helmet	s
help	ed, ing, er; s
helpful	ly, ness
helpless	ly, ness
helter-skelter	s
hem	med, ming, -line, s
her	self; s
herald	ed, ing, s
herb	age, al, alist, s
herd* (of cattle, etc.)	ed, ing, sman, s
here* (in this place)	about(s), by, with
here's (here is)	
hermit	age, -crab, s
hero	es
heroic	al, ally, s
heroine	s
heroism	
heron	s
herring	-gull, s or **herring**

ho

highway	man, men, s
hijack	ed, ing, er; s
hike	d, *d*ing, r; s
hilarious	ly, ness
hill	ock, side, top, s
hilly	ier, iest, iness
him* (he)	self
hinder	ed, ing, s
hindrance	s
hinge	d, *d*ing, s
hint	ed, ing, s
hippopotamus	es or **hippopotami**
hire* (rent)	d, *d*ing, -purchase, r; s
hiss	ed, ing, es
historic	al, ally
history	ies
hit	ting, ter; s
hitch	ed, ing, es
hitch-hike	d, *d*ing, r; s
hive	s

he's (he is; he has)
hesitate — d, éing, s
hesitation — s
hew* (chop; cut) — n, ed, ing, er, s
hexagon — al, s

hi

hibernate — d, éing, s
hibernation — s
hiccup — ed, ing, s
hid — den
hide — éing, -and-seek, away, -out, s
hideous — ly, ness
high — er;* est, ly, chair, light, -road, s
highland — er, s
Highness — es

ho

hoard* (hidden store) — ed, ing, s
hoarse* (husky) — r, st, ly, ness
hobble — d, éing, s
hobby — ies
hockey — -stick
hoe — d, ing, s
hog — skin, s
hoist — ed, ing, s
hold — ing, -all, -up, er, s
hole* (hollow place) — d, éing, s
holiday — ed, ing, -camp, -maker, s
hollow — ed, ing, ly, ness, s
holly — ies
hollyhock — s
holster — s
holy* (godly) — ier, iest, ily, iness, ies

é Drop e before adding ing

* herd	here	hew	higher	him	hoard	hoarse	hole
heard	hear	hue	hire	hymn	horde	horse	whole

hostel led, ling, ler, s
hostess es
hostile ly
hot ter, test, ly, ness, house, -plate
hotel ier, s
hound ed, ing, s
hour* (sixty mins.) ly, -hand, s
house d, ðing, hold, work, keeper, s
housemaster
housemistress es
housewife wives
hover ed, ing, port, s, craft
however
howl ed, ing, er, s

huddle d, ðing, s
hue* (colour) s

---

home -grown, -made, work, ward, s
homeless ness
homely ier, iest, ness
homesick ness
honest ly, y
honey -bee, dew, -pot, comb, suckle, s
honeymoon ed, ing, er, s
honour able, ably, ed, ing, s
hood ed, ing, s
hoof beat, mark, s or **hooves**
hook ed, ing, er, s
hooligan ism, s
hoop ed, ing, -la, s
hoot ed, ing, er, s
hop ped, ping, per, s
hope d, ðing, s
hopeful ly, ness
hopeless ly, ness
horde* (crowd) s

horizon	tal, tally, s
horn	s
hornpipe	s
hornet	s
horoscope	
horrible	ness
horribly	
horrid	ly, ness
horrify	ing
horrified	ies
horror	-stricken, struck, s
horse* (animal)	back, man, men, shoe, s
horse-chestnut	-tree, s
hose	d, *e*ing, -pipe, s
hospital	s
hospitality	
host	s
hostage	s

hug	ged, ging, s
huge	r, st, ly, ness
hullo or **hallo** or **hello**	
hum	med, ming, mer, s
human	ity, ly
humble	d, *e*ing, r, st, ness, s
humbly	
humid	ity
humiliate	d, *e*ing, s
humorous	ly, ness
humour	ed, ing, s
hump	ed, ing, s
hunch	ed, ing, es
hundred	th, weight, s
hung	
hunger	ed, ing, s
hungry	ier, iest, ily, iness
hunt	ed, ing, s

holy	horde	horse	hour	hue
wholly	hoard	hoarse	our	hew

*

e Drop e before adding ing

hy ic

hurdle	d, ∉ing, r, s
hurl	ed, ing, er, s
hurrah or **hurray**	ed, ing, s
hurricane	-lamp, s
hurry	ing
hurried	iedly, ies
hurt	ing, s
hurtle	d, ∉ing, s
husband	ed, ing, es
hush	ed, ing, es
husky	ier; iest, ily, iness
hustle	d, ∉ing, s
hutch	es

hy

hyacinth	s
hydrangea	s

id

I'd (I would; I should; I had)	
idea	s
ideal	ly, ism, ist, s
identical	ly
identification	
identify	ing
identified	ies
identity	ies
idiot	s
idiotic	al, ally
idle* (lazy)	d, ∉ing, r, st, ness, s
idly	
idol* (false god)	s
idolize	d, ∉ing, s

ig

igloo	s
ignite	d, ∉ing, s

hydraulic	ally, s
hydrofoil	s
hydrogen	
hydroplane	s
hyena or **hyaena**	s
hygiene	
hygienic	ally
hymn* (song of praise)	al, -book, s
hypnotism	s
hypnotist	s
hypnotize	d, éing, s
hysteric	al, ally, s

ic

ice	d, éing, berg, -cream, -cube, s
icicle	s
icy	ier, iest, ily, iness

ignorance	
ignorant	
ignore	d, éing, s

il

I'll (I will)	
ill	-bred, -mannered, -treated, s
illness	es
illegal	ly
illegible	
illiterate	ly, ness, s
illuminate	d, éing, s
illumination	s
illusion	ist, s
illustrate	d, éing, s
illustration	s

é Drop **e** before adding **ing**

*

hymn
him

idle
idol

im

in

im

I'm (I am)	
image	s
imaginary	
imagination	s
imagine	d, e/ing, s
imitate	d, e/ing, s
imitation	
immediate	ly, ness
immense	ly, ness
immortal	ity, ly, s
immunize	d, e/ing, s
impatience	
impatient	ly
imperfect	ion, ly
impersonate	d, e/ing, s
impersonation	s
impertinence	s

in

inaccurate	ly
inattentive	ly, ness
incapable	
inch	ed, ing, es
incident	al, ally, s
incline	d, e/ing, s
include	d, e/ing, s
inclusive	ly, ness
income	s
inconvenience	d, e/ing, s
inconvenient	ly
incorrect	ly, ness
increase	d, e/ing, s
incredible	y
incurable	
indeed	ness, s
indefinite	ly, ness
independent	ly

impertinent	ly	indicate	d, éing, s	
implement	s	indication	s	
implore	d, éing, s	indicator	s	
impolite	ly, ness	indigestion		
import	ed, ing, er, s	indignant	ly	
importance		indignation		
important	ly	indistinct	ly, ness	
impose	d, éing, s	individual	ly, s	
impossibility	ies	indoor	s	
impossible		industrial	ly	
impress	ed, ing, ive, es	industrious	ly	
impression	able, s	industry	ies	
imprison	ed, ing, ment, s	inexpensive	ly, ness	
improve	d, éing, ment, s	infant	s	
impudence		infantry	man, men	
impudent	ly	infect	ed, ing, ious, ion, s	
impure	ly	inferior	ity, ly, s	
impurity	ies	infirmary	ies	

é Drop **e** before adding **ing**

inflammable	ness
inflate	d, ing, s
influence	d, ing, s
influenza	
inform	ed, ing, ation, er, s
infrequent	ly
infuriate	d, ing, s
ingredient	s
inhabit	ed, ing, able, ant, s
inhale	d, ing, s
inherit	ed, ing, ance, s
initial	led, ling, s
inject	ed, ing, ion, s
injure	d, ing, s
injury	ies
ink	ed, ing, -bottle, -pot, stand, -well, s
inky	ier, iest, iness
inland	
inn	keeper, s

inspect	ed, ing, ion, or, s
inspiration	s
inspire	d, ing, s
install	ed, ing, ation, s
instalment	s
instance	s
instead	
instinct	ive, ively, s
institute	d, ing, s
institution	al, s
instruct	ed, ing, ive, ion, or, s
instrument	al, alist, s
insufficient	ly
insult	ed, ing, s
insurance	s
insure	d, ing, s
intact	
intelligence	aneous, ly

inner		intelligent	ly	
innings	most	intend	ed, ing, s	
innocence		intense	ly, ness	
innocent	ly, s	intent	ly, ness	
inoculate	d, ẹing, s	intention	al, ally, s	
inoculation	s	intercept	ed, ing, ive, ion, or, s	
inquire or enquire	d, ẹing, r, s	interest	ed, ing, s	
inquiry or enquiry	ies	interfere	d, ẹing, nce, s	
inquisitive	ly, ness	interior	s	
insane	ly	interlude	s	
inscription	s	intermediate	ly	
insect	s	international	ly	
insensible		interpret	ed, ing, ation, er, s	
insert	ed, ing, ion, s	interrogate	d, ẹing, s	
inside	s	interrupt	ed, ing, ion, s	
insist	ed, ing, ence, ent, s	interval	s	
insolence		intervene	d, ẹing, s	
insolent	ly	interview	ed, ing, er, s	

ẹ Drop **e** before adding ing

ir is

introduce	d, ing, s
introduction	s
intrude	d, ing, r, s
invalid	d, ing, r, s
invasion	ed, ing, s
invent	ed, ing, ive, ion, or, s
investigate	d, ing, s
investigation	s
investigator	s
invisible	ness
invitation	s
invite	d, ing, s
involve	d, ing, s
inward	ly, s

ir	
iris	es
iron	ed, ing, monger, work, s

it iv ja

it	
italic	s
itch	ed, ing, es
itchy	ier, iest, iness
item	s
its* (belonging to it)	
it's* (it is)	
itself	

iv	
I've (I have)	
ivory	ies
ivy	ies

ja	
jab	bed, bing, s
jabber	ed, ing, s

ironing-board			
irregular	ity, ly		
irrigate	d, e̸ing, s		
irrigation			
irritable	y		
irritability	ies		
irritate	d, e̸ing, s		
irritation			
is			
island	er, s		
isle* (island)	s		
isn't (is not)			
isolate	d, e̸ing, s		
isolation	d, e̸ing, s		

isle	its
aisle	it's
*	

jack	ed, ing, pot, s
jackdaw	s
jacket	s
jade	d, e̸ing, s
jagged	ly, ness
jaguar	s
jail or **gaol**	ed, ing, er, s
jam	med, ming, my, -pot, -jar, s
jamboree	s
jangle	d, e̸ing, s
January	
jar	red, ring, ful, s
jaunt	ed, ing, s
jaunty	ier, iest, ily, iness
javelin	s
jaw	-bone, s
jay	s
jazz	ed, ing, y, es

e̸ Drop **e** before adding **ing**

je ji jo

je	
jealous	ly
jealousy	ies
jeans	
jeep	s
jeer	ed, ing, s
jelly	ied, ies
jelly-fish	es or **jelly-fish**
jemmy	ies
jerk	ed, ing, s
jerky	ier, iest, ily, iness
jerkin	s
jersey	s
jest	ed, ing, er, s
jet	ted, ting, -liner, -plane, -fighter, s
jettison	ed, ing, s
jetty	ies
Jew*	ish, s
jewel*	led, ling, ler, -case, s
jewellery or **jewelry**	

ju

jog	ged, ging, ger, s
join	ed, ing, ery, er, s
joint	ed, ing, ly, s
joist	s
joke	d, ◊ing, r, s
jollity	ies
jolly	ier, iest, ily, iness
jolt	ed, ing, s
jonquil	s
jostle	d, ◊ing, s
jot	ted, ting, ter, s
journal	ism, ist, s
journey	ed, ing, s
joust	ed, ing, s
jovial	ity, ly
joy	s
joyful	ly, ness
joyous	ly, ness

ji		
jiffy	ies	
jig	ged, ging, ger, s	
jigsaw puzzle	s	
jilt	ed, ing, s	
jingle	d, é-ing, -jangle, s	
jiu-jitsu or ju-jitsu or judo		
jive	d, é-ing, s	

jo		
job	less, s	
jockey	s	
jocular	ity, ly	
jodhpurs	s	

* jew   jewel
   dew   dual
   due   duel

ju		
jubilant	ly	
jubilation	s	
jubilee	s	
judge	d, é-ing, s	
judg(e)ment	s	
judo or ju-jitsu or jiu-jitsu		
juggle	d, é-ing, r, s	
juice	s	
juicy	ier, iest, ily, iness	
july	s	
jumble	d, é-ing, -sale, s	
jump	ed, ing, er, -jet, s	
jumper	s	
jumpy	ier, iest, ily, iness	
junction	s	
june	s	
jungle	s	

é Drop e before adding ing

junior	s
junk	-shop, s
junket	s
juror	s
jury	ies
just	ly, ness
justice	
justify	ing
justified	ies
jut	ted, ting, s
juvenile	s

ka

kaleidoscope	s
kangaroo	s
karate	
kayak	s

ki

kick	ed, ing, -off, er, s
kid	skin, s
kidnap	ped, ping, per, s
kidney	-bean, s
kill	ed, ing, er, s
kiln	s
kilogram(me)	s
kilometre	s
kilt	s
kimono	s
kin	sfolk, sman, smen
kind	er, est, -hearted, s
kindly	ier, iest, ily, iness
kindness	es
kindergarten	
kindle	d, ing, s
king	dom, cup, fisher, s
kink	ed, ing, y, s

ke

keel	s
keen	er, est, ly, ness
keep	ing, er, sake, s
kennel	-maid, s
kept	
kerb* (pavement edge)	side, stone, s
kernel* (nut; seed)	s
kestrel	s
ketchup	
kettle	-holder, ful, s
key*	hole, -ring, s

kiosk	s
kipper	s
kiss	ed, ing, es
kit	ted, ting, -bag, s
kitchen	ette, -maid, s
kite	s
kitten	s

kh

| khaki | s |

kn

knack	s
knapsack	s
knave* (rogue)	s
knead* (work dough)	ed, ing, s
knee	-deep, -high, -cap, s
kneel	ed, ing, s
knelt or kneeled	
knew* (know)	

Drop e before adding ing

| * | kerb | kernel | key | knead | knave | knew |
| | curb | colonel | quay | need | nave | new |

la

knife d, d/ing, -edge, -point, **knives**
knight* (Sir) ed, ing, ly, -errant, hood, s
knit ted, ting, ter, s
knitting-needle s
knob s
knobbly ier, iest, iness
knock ed, ing, er, -out, s
knot* (tied string; sea speed) ted, ting, s
knotty ier, iest, ily, iness
know* (understand) n, ing, ingly, s
knowledge able
knuckle d, d/ing, -bone, -duster, s

la

label led, ling, s
laboratory ies
labour ed, ing, er, s
lace d, d/ing, s

land ed, ing, mark, scape, slide, slip, s
landlady ies
landlord s
lane* (narrow road) s
language s
lantern s
lap ped, ping, s
lapel s
lapse d, d/ing, s
larch es
lard ed, ing, s
larder s
large r, st, ly, ness
lark s
larva* (insect grub) e
lash ed, ing, es
lass es
lasso ed, ing, es or s
last ed, ing, ly, s

lack	ed, ing, s	**latch**	ed, ing, es
lacquer	ed, ing, s	**late**	r, st, ly, ness
lacrosse		**lathe**	s
ladder	ed, ing, s	**lather**	ed, ing, s
laden		**latitude**	s
lady	ies	**latter**	ly
ladybird	s	**laugh**	able, ed, ing, s
lag	ged, ging, gard, s	**laughter**	
lagoon	s	**launch**	ed, ing, es
laid		**launder**	ette, ed, ing, s
lain* (lie flat)		**laundress**	es
lair* (den)	s	**laundry**	ies
lake	s	**laurel**	s
lamb	ed, ing, -chop, kin, skin, swool, s	**lava*** (volcanic rock)	s
lame	d, éing, r, st, ly, ness, s	**lavatory**	ies
lament	ed, ing, able, ation, s	**lavender**	
lamp	light, -post, shade, -standard, s	**law**	ful, less, -breaker, -court, s
lance	d, éing, -corporal, r, s	**lawyer**	s

				é Drop e before adding ing	
* knight	knot	know	lain	lair	larva
night	not	no	lane	layer	lava

le

lawn -mower; -sprinkler; s
lay ing, about, -by, out, er; s
laid
layer* (coat; thickness) ed, ing; s
laze d, *d*ing; s
lazy ier, iest, ily, iness

le

lead* (metal) ed, en, -poisoning, s
lead (be first) ing, er; s
leaf ed, ing, less, -stalk, **leaves**
leafy ier, iest, iness
leaflet s
league s
leak* (hole; crack) age, ed, ing; s
leaky ier, iest, iness
lean er, est, ly, ness
lean ed, ing; s

li

lend ing, er; s
length s
lengthen ed, ing; s
lengthy ier, iest, ily, iness
lenient ly
lens es
lent* (lend)
leopard skin, s
leotard s
leper s
leprosy
less er
lessen* (make smaller) ed, ing; s
lesson* (thing learnt) s
let ting, s
let's (let us)
letter ed, ing, -writer; s
letter-box es
lettuce s

l (continued)

leant* or **leaned**	
leap	ed, ing, frog, -year, s
leapt or **leaped**	
learn	ed, ing, er, s
learnt or **learned**	
least	
leather	y, s
leave	d, *ing, r, s
lecture	d, *ing, r, s
led* (guided)	
ledge	s
leek* (vegetable)	s
left	
leg	ged, ging, less, -iron, -rest, s
legend	ary, s
legion	s
leisure	ly
lemon	ade, -drop, -juice, -peel, -tree, s

level	led, ling, -crossing, s
lever	age, ed, ing, s

li

liable	
liar* (one who lies)	s
liberal	s
liberty	ies
librarian	s
library	ies
licence* (noun)	s
license* (verb)	d, *ing, s
lick	ed, ing, er, s
licorice or **liquorice**	
lie	d, s
lying	
lieutenant	-colonel, -general, s

---

* Drop e before adding ing

*						
layer	lead	leak	leant	lessen	liar	licence
lair	led	leek	lent	lesson	lyre	license

lo

life	less, like, line, long, size, time, **lives**
life	boat, belt, -guard, -jacket, -saving
lift	ed, ing, er, s
light	er, est, ly, ness, weight, s
light	ed, ing, ish, er; house, ship, s
lighten	ed, ing, s
lightning	-conductor
like	able, d, ing, ness, s
likely	ier, iest, ihood
lilac	-tree, s
lily	ies
limb	less, s
lime	-juice, light, -tree, s
limit	ed, ing, less, s
limp	ed, ing, er, est, ly, ness, s
limpet	s
line	d, ing, sman, smen, s
linen	s
liner	s

lo

load	ed, ing, er, s
loaf	**loaves**
loan* (lend)	ed, ing, s
loathe	d, ing, s
loathsome	ly, ness
lob	bed, bing, ber, s
lobby	ies
lobster	-pot, s
local	ly, s
locality	ies
locate	d, ing, s
location	s
lock	ed, ing, er, smith, s
locket	s
locomotive	s
locust	s
lodge	d, ing, r, s
loft	s

linger	ed, ing, er, s
link	ed, ing, s
linoleum or **lino**	s
lion	-tamer; s
lioness	es
lip	-reading, stick, s
liquid	s
liquorice or **licorice**	s
list	ed, ing, s
listen	ed, ing, er; s
lit or **lighted**	
literature	
litter	ed, ing, -basket, -bin, -bug, -lout, s
little	ness
live	d, éing, r, s
lively	ier; iest, ily, iness
liver	ish, s
lizard	s

lofty	ier; iest, ily, iness
log	ged, ging, -book, -cabin, s
loganberry	ies
loiter	ed, ing, er; s
loll	ed, ing, er; s
lollipop	s
lolly	ies
lone* (alone)	
lonely	r, some / ier; iest, ily, iness
long	ed, ing, ingly, er; est, bow, -stop, s
longitude	s
look	ed, ing, er, -out, s
looking-glass	es
loom	ed, ing, s
loop	ed, ing, hole, s
loose	r, st, ly, ness
loosen	ed, ing, er; s
loot* (plunder)	ed, ing, er; s

é Drop e before adding ing

*	
loan	loot
lone	lute

lu

lop	ped, ping, -sided, s
lord	ship, s
lorry	ies
lose	*e*ing, r, s
loss	es
lost	
lotion	s
lotto	
loud	er, est, ish, ly, ness, -speaker
lounge	d, *e*ing, r, s
lout	ish, s
love	d, *e*ing, r, bird, -letter, -song, s
lovely	ier, iest, ily, iness
low	er, est, ly, ness, s
lower	ed, ing, s
lowland	er, s
loyal	ist, ly, ty
lozenge	s

ly ma

luncheon	s
lung	s
lunge	d, *e*ing, s
lupin	s
lurch	ed, ing, es
lure	d, *e*ing, s
lurk	ed, ing, er, s
luscious	ly, ness
lustre	ous
lusty	ier, iest, ily, iness
lute* (musical instrument)	s
luxuriant	ly
luxurious	ly, ness
luxury	ies

ly

lying	
lynch	ed, ing, es

lynx	s
lyre* (musical instrument)	al, s
lyric	

ma

macaroni	
mace	-bearer; s
machine	d, éing, -gun, s
machinery	
machinist	s
mackerel	s or **mackerel**
mackintosh	es
mad	der, dest, ly, ness, house, man, men
madden	ed, ing, s
madam	s
madame (French)	**mesdames**

lu

lubricate	d, éing, s
lubrication	
luck	less
lucky	ier, iest, ily, iness
ludo	
lug	ged, ging, s
luggage	-carrier, -rack, -van
lukewarm	ly, ness
lull	ed, ing, s
lullaby	ies
lumbago	s
lumber	ed, ing, er, jack, -room, s
luminous	ly, ness
lump	ed, ing, s
lumpy	ier, iest, ily, iness
lunatic	s
lunch	ed, ing, -box, es

é Drop e before adding ing

| * | lute | lyre |
| | loot | liar |

made* (make)	
magazine	s
maggot	y, s
magic	al, ally
magician	s
magistrate	ic, ically, ism, s
magnet	d, €ing, s
magnetize	ly
magnificent	ing
magnify	ies
magnified	
magpie	
maid* (girl)	en, servant, s
mail* (armour; post)	ed, ing, -bag, s
maim	ed, ing, s
main* (chief)	ly, land, stay, s
maintain	ed, ing, s
maison(n)ette	
maize* (corn)	

maniac	s
manicure	d, €ing, s
manner* (way; behaviour)	ed, s
manoeuvre	d, €ing, s
manor* (lord's land)	-house, s
mansion	s
mantelpiece	
manual	ly, s
manufacture	d, €ing, r, s
manure	d, €ing, s
manuscript	s
many	
map	ped, ping, per, -reading, s
marble	s
March	es
march	ed, ing, es
mare* (female horse)	s
margarine	s
margin	

majesty	ic, ically, ies	marigold	s
major	ette, -general, s	marine	r, s
majority	ies	marionette	s
make	éing, -believe, shift, -up, r, s	mark	ed, ing, sman, smen, er, s
malaria.		market	ed, ing, -day, -place, -stall, s
male* (man; masculine)	s	marmalade	
mallet	s	maroon	ed, ing, s
mammal	s	marquee	s
mammoth		marriage	s
man	ned, ning, hole, hood, **men**	marry	ies
manly	ier, iest, ily, iness	married	
manage	d, éing, able, ably, ment, s	marrow	s
manager	s	Mars	
manageress	es	marsh	es
mandolin	s	marshy	ier, iest, iness
mane* (hair)	s	marshal	led, ling, s
manger	s	marsh-mallow	s
mangle	d, éing, s	martyr	ed, ing, dom, s

					é Drop e before adding ing
					mare
				manner	mayor
				manor	
made	mail	main	maize		
maid	male	mane	maze		
*					

me

meadow	s
meagre	ly, ness
meal	-time, s
mean	er, est, ly, ness, s
meaning	less, s
meant	
meantime	
meanwhile	
measles	
measure	d, £ing, ment, s
meat* (flesh)	y, -axe, -ball, -pie, s
mechanic	al, ally, s
mechanism	s
mechanize	d, £ing, s
medal* (badge—for bravery, etc.)	s
medallion	s
meddle* (interfere)	d, £ing, some, r, s
medi(a)eval	

marvel	led, ling, s
marvellous	ly, ness
marzipan	
mascot	s
masculine	
mash	ed, ing, es
mask	ed, ing, s
mason	ry, s
masquerade	d, £ing, r, s
mass	ed, ing, es
massacre	d, £ing, s
massage	d, £ing, s
masseur	s
masseuse	s
massive	ly, ness
mast	ed, -head, s
master	ed, ing, ly, y, mind, piece, s
mat	ted, ting, s
matador	s

match	ed, ing, sticks, wood, box, es
mate	d, ding, s
material	s
mathematic	al, ally, ian, s
matinée	s
matron	s
matter	ed, ing, s
mattress	es
maul	ed, ing, s
mauve	r, st, s
maximum	a
may	be
May	s
maypole	s
mayonnaise	s
mayor* (head of town or city)	s
mayoress	es
maze* (puzzle)	s

medical	ly, s
medicine	s
Mediterranean	
medium	s or media
meek	er, est, ly, ness
meet* (come together)	ing, s
megaphone	s
melody	ious, iously, ies
melon	s
melt	ed, ing, s
member	s
memorial	ship, s
memorize	d, ding, s
memory	ies
menace	d, ding, s
menagerie	s
mend	ed, ing, er, s
mental	ity, ly

é Drop e before adding ing

| * | maze | mayor | meat | medal |
| | maize | mare | meet | meddle |

mi

mention	ed, ing, s
menu	s
merchant	s
merciful	ly, ness
merciless	ly, ness
mercy	ies
mere	ly
meringue	s
merit	ed, ing, s
mermaid	s
merry	ier, iest, ily, iness
mesmerize	d, 𝑒ing, s
mess	ed, ing, es
messy	ier, iest, ily, iness
message	s
messenger	s
metal	lic, work, -detector, s
meteor	ic, ite, oid, ology, ologist, s

might	ier, iest, ily, iness
mighty	d, 𝑒ing, s
migrate	s
migration	s
mild	er, est, ly, ness
mildew	ed, 𝑒ing, s
mile	age, stone, s
military	
milk	ed, ing, er, man, men, -shake, s
milky	ier, iest, ily, iness
mill	ed, ing, er, -pond, stone, s
millimetre	s
million	th, s
millionaire	s
millionairess	es
mime	d, 𝑒ing, s
mimic	ked, king, s
mince	d, 𝑒ing, er, meat, -pie, s
mind*	ed, ing, er, ful, less, -reader, s

mi

meter* (measuring box)	s
method	s
methylated spirit(s)	
metre* (length measure)	s
mew	ed, ing, s

miaow	ed, ing, s
mice	
microphone	s
microscope	s
midday	
middle	-aged, -class
midge	s
midget	s
midnight	
midst	
midway	

mine	d,* *e*ing, field, sweeper, s
miner* (mine worker)	s
mineral	s
mingle	d, *e*ing, s
miniature	a
minimum	
minister	s
minnow	s
minor* (young person; lesser)	s
minstrel	s
mint	ed, ing, y, -sauce, s
minus	es
minute (small)	-hand, s
minute (small)	ly, ness
miracle	s
miraculous	ly, ness
mirage	s
mirror	ed, ing, s

e Drop **e** before adding *ing*

	miner
	minor

meter	mind
metre	mined

*

mo

mirth	
misbehave	d, ℓing, s
misbehaviour	
mischief	-maker
mischievous	ly, ness
miser	ly, s
miserable	y
misery	ies
misfortune	s
mishap	s
mislay	ing, s
mislaid	
misplace	d, ℓing, s
miss	ed,* ing, es
missile	s
mission	s
missionary	ies
mist* (haze; fog)	ed, ing, s
misty	ier; iest, ily, iness

mockery	ies
model	led, ling, ler, s
moderate	d, ℓing, ly, ness, s
modern	ity, ly, ness, s
modernize	d, ℓing, s
modest	ly, y
moist	ure, ly, ness
moisten	ed, ing, s
mole	hill, skin, s
moment	s
monarch	s
monastery	ies
Monday	s
money	-lender; -order; -spider; s
mongrel	s
monitor	s
monitress	es
monk	s
monkey	-nut, s

mistake	n, éing, s
mistook	
mistletoe	
mistress	es
mistrust	ed, ing, s
mitten	s
mix	ed, ing, es
mixer	s
mixture	s

moan* (groan)	ed, ing, er, s
moat	ed, s
mob	bed, bing, s
mobile	s
moccasin	s
mock	ed, ing, s

monotonous	ly, ness
monster	s
month	s
monthly	ies
monument	s
mood	
moody	ier, iest, ily, iness
moon	beam, less, light, s
moor	hen, land, s
moor	age, ed, ing, s
mop	ped, ping, per, head, s
moral	ly, s
more	over
morning* (a.m.)	s
morsel	s
mortal	ly, s
mortar	s
mosaic	s

é Drop e before adding ing

missed	moan	morning
mist	mown	mourning
*		

mu

mosquito	es
moss	es
mossy	ier, iest, iness
motel	ly
moth	s
moth	-eaten, -proof, ball, s
mother	ed, ing, less, ly, hood, s
motion	ed, ing, less, -picture, s
motor	ed, ing, -bike, -boat, -car, ist, s
motor	-cycle, -cyclist, -scooter, way, s
motto	es
mould	ed, ing, er, s
mouldy	ier, iest, iness
moult	ed, ing, s
mount	s
mount	ed, ing, s
mountain	ous, side, -top, s
mountaineer* (sorrowing)	ing, s
mourning* (sorrowing)	ed, ful, fully, er, s

my

multiply	ing
multiplied	ier, ies
multitude	s
mumble	d, d'ing, r, s
mummy	ies
mumps	
munch	ed, ing, es
mural	s
murder	ed, ing, er, s
murderess	es
murmur	ed, ing, er, s
muscle* (of body)	
museum	s
mushroom	s
music	al, ally, -case, -hall, -stand
musician	s
musket	eer; -shot, s
mussel* (shellfish)	
must	

mouse

mouse	d, *e*ing, *e*y, r; -hole, trap, **mice**
moustache	s
mouth	-organ, ful, s
movable	s
move	d, *e*ing, r, ment, s
mow	s
mown* (cut grass, etc.)	ed, ing, er, s

mu

much	
mud	-bank, -bath, -flat, guard
muddy	ier, iest, ily, iness
muddle	d, *e*ing, r, s
muffle	d, *e*ing, r, s
mulberry	ies
mule	teer; s
multiplication	

mustn't (must not)	
mustard	-pot
musty	ier, iest, ily, iness
mutineer	s
mutiny	ing
mutinied	ies
mutter	ed, ing, er, s
mutton	-chop, -cutlet
muzzle	d, *e*ing, s

my

myrrh	
myself	
mystery	ies
mysterious	ly, ness
mystify	ing
mystified	ies

e Drop e before adding ing

*	mourning
	morning
	mown
	moan
	muscle
	mussel

na

nail	ed, ing, -scissors, -file, s
naked	ly, ness
name	d, éing, ly, less, -plate, sake, s
nanny	ies
napkin	-ring, s
nappy	ies
narcissus	es or **narcissi**
narrate	d, éing, s
narrow	ed, ing, er, est, ish, ly, ness, s
nasturtium	s
nasty	ier, iest, ily, iness
nation	al, ally, wide, s
nationality	ies
native	s
nativity	ies
natural	ly, ness
naturalist	s
nature	s

ne

needle	work, -case, s
negative	s
neglect	ed, ing, s
neglectful	ly, ness
Negress	es
Negro	es
neigh	ed, ing, s
neighbour	ing, ly, hood, s
neither	
nephew	s
nerve	d, éing, -racking, s
nervous	ly, ness
nest	ed, ing, -egg, ful, s
nestle	d, éing, s
net	ted, ting, ball, ful, s
nettle	s
neutral	s
never	more, theless
new* (just made)	er, est, ly, ness

naughty ier, iest, ily, iness
nautical ly
naval
nave* (main part of church) s
navigate d, éing, s
navigation
navigator s
navy ies

ne

near ed, ing, er, est, ly, ness, s
neat er, est, ly, ness
necessary ily, ies
necessity ies
neck lace, let, line, tie, s
need* (want) ed, ing, s
needn't (need not)

*	nave	need
	knave	knead
	nave	need

---

news -aster, -letter, -reel, -sheet, y
newsagent
newspaper man, men, -boy, -girl, s
newt s
next

ni

nibble d, éing, r, s
nice r, st, ly, ness
nick ed, ing, s
nickname d, éing, s
niece s
night* -club, fall, -light, mare, -time, s
nightingale s
nil
nimble r, st, ness, -footed
nimbly

é Drop e before adding ing

night	new
knight	knew

no

no* (not any; opp. of yes)	es
noble	r, st, man, men, s
nobody	ies
nod	ded, ding, der, s
noise	less, lessly, s
noisy	ier, iest, ily, iness
nomad	ic, s
none* (not any)	
nonsense	
noodle	s
noon	day
noose	s
Norman	ly
north	-east, -west, -ern, erly, wards
nose	d, éing, bag, bleed, dive, gay, s
nostril	s
not* (no)	

nu

nuclear	s
nude	s
nudist	s
nudge	d, éing, s
nugget	s
nuisance	s
numb	ed, ing, ly, ness, s
number	ed, ing, -plate, s
numeral	s
numerical	ly
numerous	ly
nun* (religious woman)	s
nurse	d, éing, maid, s
nursery	ies
nut	ted, ting, cracker, shell, -tree, s
nutty	ier, iest, ily, iness
nuthatch	es
nutmeg	s

notable		al, ist
notch	ed, ing, es	
note	d, éing, book, case, paper, let, s	
nothing		
notice	d, éing, able, ably, -board, s	
notify	ing	
notified	ication, ies	
notion	s	
nougat	s	
nought		
nourish	ment, ed, ing, es	
novel	ist, s	
novelty	ies	
November		
novice	s	
now	adays	
nowhere		
nozzle	s	

nutrition		al, ist
nutritious		ly, ness
nuzzle		d, éing, s
	ny	
nylon		s
nymph		s
	oa	
oaf* (stupid person)		ish, s or **oaves**
oak		-apple, -tree, s
oar* (rowing blade)		sman, smen, s
oasis		es
oast		-house, s
oat		meal, cake, s
oath* (promise; swear-word)		s

é Drop **e** before adding ing

*	no	none	not		oaf	oar
	know	nun	knot		oath	ore
						or

ob oc

ob

obedience	
obedient	ly
obey	ed, ing, s
object	ed, ing, or, s
objection	able, ably, s
obligation	s
oblige	d, éing, s
obliterate	d, éing, s
oblong	s
oboe	s
obscure	ést, s
obscurity	d, éing, ly, s
observant	ly
observation	s
observatory	ies
observe	d, éing, r, s
obstacle	-course, -race, s
obstinate	ly

od of og oi ol

od

odd	er, est, ly, ness, ment, s
odious	ly, ness
odour	s

of

of	
off	ing, hand, chance, -side, spring
offence	s
offend	ed, ing, er, s
offensive	ly, ness
offer	ed, ing, s
offertory	ies
office	-block, -boy, -girl, -worker, s
officer	s
official	ly, s
often	er, est

obstruct	ed, ing, ion, s
obtain	able, ed, ing, s
obvious	ly, ness

oc

occasion	al, ally, s
occupant	s
occupation	s
occupy	ing
occupied	ier; ies
occur	red, ring, rence, s
ocean	s
o'clock	
octagon	al, s
October	
octopus	es or **octopuses**
oculist	s

—

	pipe, ist, s
	s
	d, ding, s

ental

oil	ed,
oil	-heater,
oily	
ointment	s

ol

old	en, er, est, ish, -time
old-fashioned	ness
olive	-oil, -grove, -tree, s
Olympic Games or **Olympics**	

é Drop **e** before adding **ing**

om on op

om

omelet(te)	s
omen	s
omission	s
omit	ted, ting, s
omnibus	es

on

once	
oncoming	self, -sided, s
one*	y, -skin, s
onion	s
onlooker	s
only	
onslaught	s
onto	s
onward	s

or os ot

or

oral	ly
orange	ade, -blossom, -peel, -tree, s
orang-(o)utan	s
orator	s
orbit	ed, ing, s
orchard	s
orchestra	l, s
orchid	s
ordeal	s
order	ed, ing, s
orderly	iness, ies
ordinary	ily, iness
ore* (metal in rock)	s
organ	-grinder, -loft
organization	
organize	s
orient	
ori	

op

opal	s
opaque	ly, ness
open	ed, ing, ly, ness, er, s
opera	-glasses, -house, -singer, s
operatic	s
operate	d, e'ing, s
operation	s
operator	s
opinion	s
opponent	s
opportunity	ies
oppose	d, e'ing, s
opposite	s
opposition	s
optician	ly, ness
optimist	ic, ically, s

---

origin		s
original		ity, ly
originate		d, e'ing, s
ornament		ed, ing, al, ation, s
ornithologist		
ornithology		
orphan		ed, ing, age, s
osier	**os**	s
ostrich		es
other	**ot**	s
otherwise		
otter		s

e' Drop e before adding ing

* one (I)   ore
   won   oar
            or

ou ov   ow ox oy

ou	
ought	
ounce	s
our* (belonging to us)	s
ourselves	
out come, let, look, put, right, standing	
outbreak	s
outburst	s
outcast	s
outer	most
outfit	ted, ting, ter, s
outhouse	s
outing	s
outlaw	ed, ing, s
outline	d, éing, s
outnumber	ed, ing, s
out-patient	s
outpost	s
outrage	d, éing, s

overdose	d, éing, s
overflow	ed, ing, s
overhaul	ed, ing, s
overhead	s
overhear	ing, s
overheard	
overjoyed	
overlap	ped, ping, s
overload	ed, ing, s
overlook	ed, ing, s
overpower	ed, ing, s
overseas	
oversleep	ing, s
overslept	
overtake	n, éing, s
overtook	
overthrow	n, ing, s
overthrew	
overtime	

outrageous	ly, ness
outside	
outskirts	r, s
outward	ly, ness, s
outwit	ted, ting, s

ov

oval	s
oven	s
over	s
overall	s
overbalance	d, éing, s
overboard	
overcame	
overcome	éing, s
overcoat	s
overcrowd	ed, ing, s

overturn	ed, ing, s
overwhelm	ed, ing, s
overwork	ed, ing, s

ow

owe	d, éing, s
owl	et, s
own	ed, ing, er, s

ox

ox	en
oxlip	s
oxygen	

oy

oyster	-bed, -catcher, -farm, -shell, s

é Drop e before adding ing

* our
  hour

pa

pa	
pace	d, cing, r, s
Pacific	
pack	ed, ing, er, s
package	d, cing, s
packet	ed, ing, s
pad	ded, ding, der, s
paddle	d, cing, r, -boat, -steamer, s
padlock	ed, ing, s
page	s
pageant	-boy, s
paid	
pail* (bucket)	ful, s
pain* (suffering)	ed, ing, -killer, s
painful	ly, ness
painless	ly, ness
paint	ed, ing, er, s
pair* (two)	ed, ing, s
palace	s

parachute	d, cing, -troops, s
parade	d, cing, -ground, s
paraffin	-heater, -oil
parallel	ed, ing, s
paralyse	d, cing, s
paralysis	es
paratroops	
parcel	led, ling, s
parch	ed, ing, es
parchment	s
pardon	able, ed, ing, s
pare* (cut away; peel)	d, cing, s
parent	age, al, s
parish	es
park	ed, ing, land, -keeper, s
parliament	s
parrot	s
parsley	-sauce
parsnip	s

pale* (faint; whitish)	r, st, ly, ness, s
palette	s
palm	-tree, s
pamper	ed, ing, er, s
pamphlet	s
pan	ned, ning, ful, cake, s
panda	s
pane* (sheet of glass)	s
panel	led, ling, list, s
panic	ked, king, ky, -stricken, -struck, s
panorama	s
pansy	ies
pant	ed, ing, s
panther	s
pantomime	s
pantry	ies
paper	ed, ing, -boy, -girl, -chain, -clip, s
papier mâché	

parson	age, s
part	ed, ing, ly, s
particle	s
particular	ly, s
partition	ed, ing, s
partner	ed, ing, ship, s
partridge	s
party	ies
pass	ed,* ing, able, es
passage	way, s
passenger	s
passion	ate, ately, s
passport	s
password	s
past* (time gone by)	
paste	d, ẻing, s
pastel* (crayon)	
pastille* (sweet)	

				ẻ Drop e before adding ing
pail	pain	pair	passed	pastel
pale	pane	pare	past	pastille
*		pear		

pe

pastime s
pastry ies
pasture d, ∉ing, s
pasty ies
pat ted, ting, s
patch ed, ing, work, es
patchy ier, iest, ily, iness
path way, s
pathetic ally
patience
patient ly, s
patrol led, ling, man, men, -leader, s
patter ed, ing, s
pattern ed, ing, -book, s
pause* (hesitate) d, ∉ing, s
pave d, ∉ing, ment, s
pavilion s
paw (animal's foot) s,* ed, ing
pawn ed, ing, broker, shop, -ticket, s

peck ed, ing, er, s
peculiar ly
peculiarity ies
pedal* (foot-lever) led, ling, -cycle, s
peddle* (to hawk goods) d, ∉ing, s
pedestrian s
pedigree s
pedlar s
peel* (skin of fruit) ed, ing, er, s
peep ed, ing, er, -hole, -show, s
peer* (stare) ed, ing, s
peg ged, ging, s
Pekin(g)ese **Pekin(g)ese**
pelican s
pellet s
pelt ed, ing, s
pen ned, ning, -friend, -nib, s
penalty ies
pence

pay	able, ing, er, ment, -day, -desk, s
paid	

pe

pea	nut, -pod, -soup, -shooter, s
peace* (quiet)	able, -offering, -time
peaceful	ly, ness
peach	es
peacock	s
peahen	s
peak	ed, ing, s
peal* (sound of bells)	ed, ing, s
pear* (fruit)	-drop, -tree, s
pearl	-diver, -fisher, s
peasant	ry, s
peat	-bog, -moor, y
pebble	-stone, s
pebbly	ier, iest, iness

pencil	led, ling, -case, -sharpener, s
pendulum	s
penetrate	d, ing, s
penguin	s
peninsula	s
penknife	knives
pennant	s
penny	ies or **pence**
penniless	ly, ness
pension	ed, ing, able, er, -book, s
people	s
pepper	ed, ing, y, -pot, mint, s
perambulator	s
perch	ed, ing, es
percussion	-band, s
perfect	ly, ed, ing, ion, s
perform	ed, ing, ance, er, s
perfume	d, ing, s

e Drop e before adding ing

* pause	peace	pear	peal	pedal	peer
paws	piece	pair	peel	peddle	pier
		pare			

ph

perhaps	
peril	ous, ously, s
period	ic, ical, ically, s
periscope	s
perish	ed, ing, es
permanent	ly
permission	
permit	ted, ting, s
perplex	ed, ing, es
persevere	d, ďing, ďance, s
persist	ed, ing, ence, ent, s
person	al, ally, s
perspiration	
perspire	d, ďing, s
persuade	d, ďing, s
persuasion	
persuasive	ly, ness
pessimist	ic, ically, s
pester	ed, ing, s

pi

pi* (π = 3.14159)	
pianist	s
piano	-accordion, -stool, s
piccolo	-player, s
pick	ed, ing, er, axe, pocket, s
pickle	d, ďing, r, s
picnic	ked, king, ker, -basket, s
picture	d, ďing, -book, -frame, s
picturesque	ly, ness
pie*	crust, -shop, s
piece* (a part)	d, ďing, s
pier** (jetty)	s
pierce	d, ďing, s
pierrot	s
pig	let, skin, s
pigsty	ies
pigeon	-hole, -house, -loft, s
pigmy or pygmy	ies

pet	ted, ting, -shop, s
petal	s
petrol	eum, -pump, -station, s
petticoat	s
pew	s
pewter	s

ph

phantom	s
pheasant	s
philatelist	s
phone	d, eing, -booth, s
photo	-fit, -frame, s
photograph	ed, ing, y, er, s
physical	ly
physician	s
physics	

pigtail	s
pike	man, men, staff, s
pilchard	s
pile	d, eing, s
pilgrim	age, s
pillar	s
pillar-box	es
pillion	-rider, -seat, s
pillow	case, slip, -fight, s
pilot	ed, ing, s
pimple	d, eing, s
pimply	ier, iest, iness
pin	ned, ning, cushion, s
pincers	**pincers**
pinch	ed, ing, es
pine	d, eing, apple, -cone, -needle, -tree, s
pink	er, est, ish, y, ness, s
pint	s

e Drop e before adding ing

pi	pier	piece
* pie	peer	peace

pl

pioneer	ed, ing, s
pipe	d, éing, r, -cleaner, ful, s
piranha	s
pirate	s
pistil* (part of flower)	
pistol* (small gun)	-shot, s
pit	ted, ting, fall, -head, -prop, s
pitch	ed, ing, -black, -dark, es
pitchfork	ed, ing, s
piteous	ly
pity	ing
pitied	iful, iless, ies
pixie	s or **pixy**, ies
pizza	s

pl

placard	s
place* (position)	d, ing, s
plague	d, éing, s

po

plead	ed, ing, s
pleasant	ly, ness
please	d, éing, s
pleasure	s
pleat	ed, ing, s
plentiful	ly, ness
plenty	
pliers	**pliers**
	s
plimsoll	s
plod	ded, ding, der, s
plot	ted, ting, ter, s
plough	ed, ing, man, men, boy, s
pluck	ed, ing, er, s
plucky	ier, iest, ily, iness
plug	ged, ging, ger, s
plum*	-pudding, -stone, -tree, s
plumage	s
plumb*	ed, ing, -line, s
plumber	s

plaice* (fish)	
plain*	er, est, ly, ness, s
plait	ed, ing, s
plan	ned, ning, ner, s
plane* (tool; to smooth)	d, éing, s
plane* (aeroplane; tree)	s
planet	s
plank	ed, ing, s
plant	ed, ing, s
plaster	ed, ing, ation, er, s
plastic	s
plasticine	
plate	d, éing, ful, -glass, -rack, s
platform	s
platinum	
play	ed, ing, ground, mate, time, er; s
play	-group, -pen, thing, wright, s
playful	ly, ness

plump	er, est, ly, ness
plunder	ed, ing, er; s
plunge	d, éing, r, s
plural	s
plus	es
po	
poach	ed, ing, es
poacher	s
pocket	ed, ing, -book, -money, ful, s
pocket-knife	-knives
podgy	ier, iest, ily, iness
poem	s
poet	ic, ical, ically, s
poetry	
point	ed, ing, -blank, -duty, less, er; s
poise	d, éing, s
poison	ed, ing, ous, ously, er; s

é Drop e before adding ing

*	pistil	place	plain	plum
	pistol	plaice	plane	plumb

poke	d, ∉ing, r, s
polar bear	s
pole* (long rod)	-jump, -vault, s
police	d, ∉ing, -officer; man, woman
police force	s
police station	s
polish	ed, ing, es
polite	r, st, ly, ness
political	ly
politician	s
poll* (vote)	ed, ing, s
pollen	
polo	-stick
polytechnic	s
polythene	
pomp	ous, ously, osity
pond	-life, -snail, -weed, s
ponder	ed, ing, s
pontoon	-bridge, s

portable	s
porter	s
porthole	s
portion	ed, ing, s
portrait	s
pose	d, ∉ing, s
position	ed, ing, s
positive	ly, ness
possess	ed, ing, ive, es
possession	s
possibility	ies
possible	
possibly	
post	ed, ing, man, men, card, mark, s
postage	-stamp
postal order	s
poster	s
post office	s
postpone	d, ∉ing, ment, s

pony	ies
poodle	s
pool	ed, ing, s
poor* (not rich)	er, est, ly, ness
pop	ped, ping, per, corn, gun, s
pop	-group, -music, -singer, -song, s
poplar	-tree, s
poppy	ies
popular	ity, ly
population	s
porcelain	
porch	es
porcupine	s
pore* (study; tiny hole)	d, ℯing, s
pork	-butcher, -chop, -pie, er, y
porpoise	s
porridge	
port	s

posy	ies
pot	ted, ting, ful, -luck, -hole, -shot, s
potato	es
potion	s
potter	ed, ing, s
pottery	ies
pouch	es
poultice	d, ℯing, s
poultry	-farm
pounce	d, ℯing, s
pound	ed, ing, s
pour* (flow out)	ed, ing, er, s
pout	ed, ing, er, s
poverty	-stricken
powder	ed, ing, y, -puff, -room, s
power	ed, -house, -plant, -station, s
powerful	ly, ness
powerless	ly, ness

ℯ Drop e before adding ing

*	pole	poor
	poll	pore
		pour

pra pre

pr

practical	ly, ity, ness
practice* (noun)	s
practise* (verb)	d, ₫ing, s
prairie	s
praise	d, ₫ing, s
prance	d, ₫ing, s
prank	ster; s
prawn	ed, ing, er; s
pray* (ask God)	ed, ing, s
prayer	-book, -meeting, s
preach	ed, ing, es
preacher	
precaution	ary; s
precious	ly, ness
precipice	s
prefect	s
prefer	red, ring, able, ably, ence, s
prehistoric	al, ally

pri pro

price	d, ₫ing, less, -list, -tag, s
prick	ed, ing, er; s
prickle	d, ₫ing, s
prickly	ier, iest, iness
pride* (proudness)	d, ₫ing, s
pried* (looked into)	
priest	ly, hood, s
priestess	es
primary school	s
primitive	ly, ness
primrose	s
prince	ly, s
princess	es
principal* (head; chief)	ly, s
principle* (rule; truth)	s
print	ed, ing, er; s
prison	er; s
private	ly, s
privilege	d, ₫ing, s

preliminary	ies		**prize**	d, éing, -winner, s
premises	s		**probability**	ies
preparation			**probable**	
prepare	d, éing, s		**probably**	
prescribe	d, éing, s		**problem**	s
prescription	s		**procedure**	
presence			**proceed**	ed, ing, s
present	ed, ing, ation, s		**process**	ed, ing, es
presently			**procession**	s
preserve	d, éing, s		**proclaim**	ed, ing, s
president			**procure**	d, éing, s
press	ed, ing, es		**prod**	ded, ding, s
pressure	-cooker; gauge, s		**produce**	d, éing, r, s
pretend	ed, ing, er, s		**product**	ive, ion, s
pretty	ier, iest, ily, iness		**profession**	al, ally, s
prevent	ed, ing, ion, s		**professor**	s
previous	ly, ness		**profit*** (gain)	able, ed, ing, eer, s
prey* (victim; thing hunted)	ed, ing, s		**programme**	d, éing, r, s

é Drop e before adding ing

		principal	profit
		principle	prophet
		pride	
		pried	
*			
practice	pray		
practise	prey		

pu

public	ly, -house
publication	s
publicity	
publish	ed, ing, es
publisher	s
pudding	s
puddle	s
puff	ed, ing, er, s
puffy	ier, iest, ily, iness
pull	ed, ing, er, s
pullover	s
pulley	ed, ing, er, s
pulp	s
pulpit	-block, s
pulse	ed, ing, er, s
pump	s
pumpkin	d, *d*ing, s
punch	ed, ing, s
	s
	ed, ing, es

pru pry

progress	ed, ing, es
prohibit	ed, ing, s
project	ed, ing, ile, ion, or, s
promenade	d, *d*ing, r, s
prominent	ly
promise	d, *d*ing, s
promote	d, *d*ing, r, s
promotion	s
prompt	ed, ing, er, est, ly, ness, s
pronounce	d, *d*ing, ment, s
proof	s
prop	ped, ping, s
propel	led, ling, ler, s
proper	ly
property	ies
prophecy (noun)	ies
prophesy (verb)	ied, ies
prophesying	
prophet* (foreteller of future)	s

proposal	s
propose	d, éing, r, s
proprietor	s
prosecute	d, éing, s
prosper	ed, ing, ous, ously, ity, s
protect	ed, ing, ion, ive, or, s
protest	ed, ing, s
Protestant	s
protrude	d, éing, s
proud	er, est, ly
prove	d, éing, s
proverb	s
provide	d, éing, r, s
provision	ed, ing, s
prowl	ed, ing, er, s
prune	d, éing, s
pry	ing
pried*	ies

punctual	ity, ly
puncture	d, éing, s
punish	able, ed, ing, es
punishment	
punt	ed, ing, er, s
pupa	e
pupil	s
puppet	ry, -play, -show, s
puppy	ies
purchase	d, éing, r, s
pure	r, st, ly
purity	
purple	r, st, ness
purpose	ly, s
purr	ed, ing, s
purse	r, -snatcher, s
pursue	d, éing, r, s
pursuit	s

é Drop e before adding ing

*	prophet	pried
	profit	pride

py qua que qui quo

push	ed, ing, es
pussy	ies
put	ting, s
putt (golf)	ed, ing, er, s
putting-green	s
putty	
puzzle	d, éing, r, ment, s

py

pygmy or **pigmy**	ies
pyjamas	
pylon	s
pyramid	s
python	s

qua

quack	ed, ing, s
quadrangle	s

que

queen	s
queer	er, est, ly, ness
quell	ed, ing, s
quench	ed, ing, es
query	ing
queried	ies
quest	ed, ing, s
question	ed, ing, er, -master, s
queue* (line of persons, etc.)	d, r, s
queueing or **queuing**	

qui

quibble	d, éing, r, s
quick	er, est, ly, ness
quicken	ed, ing, s
quiet	ed, ing, er, est, ly, ness, s
quieten	ed, ing, s

quadruplet	s
quaint	er, est, ly, ness
quake	d, éing, s
qualification	s
qualify	ing
qualified	ies
quantity	ies
quarantine	d, éing, s
quarrel	led, ling, ler, some, s
quarry	ing
quarried	ies
quart (two pints)	s*
quarter	ed, ing, s
quartet(te)	s
quartz* (rock-crystal)	s
quay* (wharf)	side, s

quill	s
quilt	ed, ing, s
quince	s
quinine	s
quintet(te)	s
quintuplet	s
quire* (measure of paper)	s
quit	ted, ting, ter, s
quite	
quiver	ed, ing, s
quiz	zed, zing, zes
quoit	s
quota	s
quotation	s
quote	d, éing, s

quo

---

*				é Drop e before adding ing
quarts	quay	queue	quire	
quartz	key	cue	choir	

ra

rabbit	ed, ing, er, -hole, -warren, s
race	d, éing, r, course, horse, track, s
rack	ed, ing, s
racket* (noise)	ed, ing, eer, s
racket* or **racquet*** (bat)	s
radar	
radiate	d, éing, s
radiator	s
radio	ed, ing, s
radish	es
radius	i
raffle	d, éing, r, -ticket, s
raft	s
rafter	s
rag	ged, ging, s
ragged	ly, ness
rage	d, éing, s
raid	ed, ing, er, s

r'ea reb

ransack	ed, ing, er, s
ransom	ed, ing, s
rap* (knock)	ped, ping, s
rapid	ity, ly, s
rare	r, st, ly, ness
rascal	ly, s
rash	er, est, ly, ness
rasher	s
raspberry	ies
rat	ted, ting, -hole, -poison, -trap, s
rate	d, éing, payer, s
rather	
ration	ed, ing, s
rattle	d, éing, r, snake, s
rave	d, éing, s
raven	s
ravenous	ly, ness
ravine	s
raw	er, est, ly, ness

			ray (beam of light)	s*
rail		ing, s	**razor**	-blade, -edge, -shell, s
railway	-carriage, -crossing, -line, s			
rain*	ed, ing, -water, bow, coat, drop, s		**re**	
rainy	ier; iest, ily, iness		**reach**	ed, ing, es
raise* (lift up)	d, e̸ing, s		**react**	ed, ing, ion, or; s
raisin	s		**read***	ing, er; s
rake	d, e̸ing, r, s		**ready**	ier; iest, ily, iness
rally	ing		**real*** (true)	ly, ist, istic, ism
rallied	ies		**reality**	ies
ram	med, ming, rod, s		**realize**	d, e̸ing, s
ramble	d, e̸ing, r, s		**really**	
ramshackle			**reap**	ed, ing, er; s
ranch	es		**reappear**	ed, ing, ance, s
rancher	s		**rear**	ed, ing, guard, -lamp, -light, ward, s
random	ly		**rearrange**	d, e̸ing, ment, s
rang			**reason**	ed, ing, able, ably, s
range	d, e̸ing, r, s		**rebel**	led, ling, s
rank	ed, ing, s			

					e̸ Drop e before adding ing
	racket	rain	raise	rap	read	read	real
*	racquet	reign	rays	wrap	reed	red	reel
		rein					

rec red ree ref

rebellion	s
rebellious	ly, ness
rebound	ed, ing, s
recall	ed, ing, s
recapture	d, éing, s
receipt	ed, ing, -book, s
receive	d, ing, r, s
recent	ly, ness
receptacle	s
reception	ist, s
recess	ed, ing, es
recipe	s
recital	s
recitation	s
recite	d, éing, s
reckless	ly, ness
reckon	ed, ing, er, s
recognize	d, éing, s
recollect	ed, ing, ion, s

reg reh rei rej rel

referee	d, ing, s
reference	-book, s
reflect	ed, ing, ion, or, s
refrain	ed, ing, s
refresh	ed, ing, es
refreshment	s
refrigerator	s
refuge	s
refugee	s
refund	ed, ing, s
refusal	s
refuse	d, éing, s
regain	ed, ing, s
regard	ed, ing, less, lessly, s
regatta	s
regiment	ed, ing, al, s
region	al, s
register	ed, ing, s
regret	ted, ting, table, tably, s

recommend	ed, ing, ation, s
record	ed, ing, -player, s
recorder	ed, ing, s
recover	ed, ing, s
recovery	ies
recreation	-ground, s
recruit	ed, ing, ment, s
rectangle	s
red* (colour)	der, dest, dish, dy, ness, s
redden	ed, ing, s
redskin	s
redecorate	d, ℮ing, s
reduce	d, ℮ing, s
reduction	s
reed* (tall grass)	-knot, s
reel* (spool; dance; stagger)	ed, ing, s
refer	red, ring, s

regretful	ly
regular	ity, ly
regulate	d, ℮ing, s
regulation	s
rehearsal	s
rehearse	d, ℮ing, s
reign* (rule)	ed, ing, s
rein* (strap)	ed, ing, s
reindeer	
reinforce	d, ℮ing, ment, s
reject	ed, ing, ion, s
rejoice	d, ℮ing, s
rejoin	ed, ing, s
relate	d, ℮ing, s
relation	s
relative	s
relax	ed, ing, es
relay	ed, ing, -race, s

℮ Drop e before adding ing

red	reed	reel	reign
read	read	real	rein
*			rain

release	d, ¢ing, s
reliable	s
relic	ness
relief	s
relieve	d, ¢ing, s
religion	s
religious	ly, ness
rely	ing
relied	iable, ies
remain	ed, ing, der, s
remark	ed, ing, able, ably, s
remedy	ies
remember	ed, ing, s
remembrance	s
remind	ed, ing, er, s
remnant	s
remote	ly, ness
removal	s
remove	d, ¢ing, r, s

require	d, ¢ing, ment, s
rescue	d, ¢ing, r, s
resemblance	s
resemble	d, ¢ing, s
reservation	s
reserve	d, ¢ing, s
reservoir	s
reside	d, ¢ing, nce, nt, s
resign	ed, ing, ation, s
resist	ed, ing, ance, s
resolution	s
resort	ed, ing, s
respect	ed, ing, able, ably, ful fully, s
responsibility	ies
responsible	
rest	ed, ing, -cure, -home, -room, s
restful	ly, ness
restless	ly, ness
restaurant	s

renew	ed, ing, able, al, s	result	ed, ing, s
rent	ed, ing, able, al, s	resume	d, *e*ing, s
repair	ed, ing, able, er, s	retire	d, *e*ing, ment, s
repay	ing, able, ment, s	retrace	d, *e*ing, s
repaid		retreat	ed, ing, s
repeat	ed, edly, ing, er, s	retrieve	d, *e*ing, r, s
repetition	s	return	ed, ing, able, -ticket, s
replace	d, *e*ing, able, ment, s	reveal	ed, ing, s
replay	ed, ing, s	revenge	d, *e*ing, s
reply	ing	reverse	d, *e*ing, s
replied	ies	review	ed, ing, s
report	ed, *e*ing, er, s	revive	d, *e*ing, s
represent	ed, ing, ative, s	revolt	ed, ing, s
reproduce	d, *e*ing, s	revolution	s
reptile	s	revolve	d, *e*ing, s
republic	an, s	revolver	s
reputation	s	reward	ed, ing, s
request	ed, ing, s		

e Drop **e** before adding **ing**

ro

ripple	d, ing, s
rise	ing, r, s
risen	
risk	ed, ing, s
risky	ier; iest, ily, iness
rissole	s
rival	led, ling, s
rivalry	ies
river	-bank, -bed, -boat, side, s
rivet	ed, ing, er; s

ro

road* (highway)	side, way, -sweeper; s
roam	ed, ing, er; s
roar	ed, ing, er; s
roast	ed, ing, er; s
rob	bed, bing, ber; s
robbery	ies

rh

rheumatism	
rhinoceros	es
rhododendron	s
rhubarb	
rhyme	d, ing, s
rhythm	ic, ical, ically, s

ri

rib	bed, bing, s
ribbon	s
rice	-pudding, -field, s
rich	er; est, ly, ness, es
rick	ed, ing, s
rickety	iness
ridden	
riddle	d, ing, r; s
ride	ing, r; s

riding -crop, -school, -stable, -whip, s	**robe** d, éing, s
ridge d, éing, s	**robin** -redbreast, s
ridicule ly, ness	**robot** s
rifle d, éing, man, men, -range, -shot, s	**rock** ed, ing, -cake, -garden, s
rig ged, ging, ger, s	**rocky** ier, iest, ily, iness
right* (true; opp. left) ful, ly, -handed, s	**rockery** ies
rigid ity, ly, ness	**rocket** ed, ing, s
rim med, ming, less, s	**rode*** (ride)
rind	**rodeo** s
ring* (circle) ed, ing, leader, -master; s	**roe*** (deer; fish eggs) s
ring* (bell sound) ing, er, s	**rogue** s
rink s	**rôle*** (actor's part) s
rinse d, éing, r, s	**roll*** (turn over) ed, ing, -call, mop, er, s
riot ed, ing, er, s	**roller-skate** d, éing, r, s
rip ped, ping, per, -cord, s	**Roman** s
ripe r, st, ly, ness	**romance** d, éing, s
ripen ed, ing, s	**romantic** ally, s
	romp ed, ing, er, s

é Drop **e** before adding *ing*

* right.	ring	road	roe	rôle
write	wring	rode	row	roll
		rowed		

ru

roof	-garden, -rack, -top, s
rook	s
rookery	ies
room	ful, s
roomy	ier, iest, ily, iness
root* (part of a plant)	ed, ing, s
rope	d, *e*ing, s
rose	-bud, -garden, -hip, -tree, wood, s
rosette	d, *e*ing, -ladder, s
rosy	ier, iest, ily, iness
rot	ted, ting, s
rotate	d, *e*ing, s
rotten	ly, ness
rough	ed, ing, er, est, ly, ness, s
roughen	ed, ing, s
round	ed, ing, ish, ness, sman, smen, s
roundabout	s
rounders	
rouse	d, *e*ing, s

sa

rude	r, st, ly, ness
ruffian	s
ruffle	d, *e*ing, s
Rugby	-ball
rugged	ly, ness
ruin	ed, ing, ous, s
rule	d, *e*ing, r, s
rumble	d, *e*ing, s
rummage	d, *e*ing, -sale, s
rumour	ed, ing, s
run	ning, ner, way, s
rung* (ring, ladder step)	s
rural	ly
rush	ed, ing, es
rust	ed, ing, less, -proof, s
rusty	ier, iest, ily, iness
rustle	d, *e*ing, r, s
rut	ted, ting, s
rutty	ier, iest, iness

route* (a way)	d, ∉ing, s
routine	s
rove	d, ∉ing, r, s
row (quarrel)	ed, ∉ing, s
row* (line; use oars)	ed, * ing, er,-boat, s
rowing-boat	s
rowdy	ier, iest, ily, iness, ies
royal	ist, ly, ty

ru

rub	bed, bing, s
rubber	-stamp, -tree, s
rubbish	-tip, -heap, y
rubble	
ruby	ies
rucksack	s
rudder	s

sa

sabbath	s
sack	ed, ing, ful, -race, s
sacred	ly, ness
sacrifice	d, ∉ing, s
sad	der, dest, ly, ness
saddle	d, ∉ing, s
sadden	ed, ing, s
safari	s
safe	d, ∉ing, r,-bag, s
safety	r, st, ly, ness, s
sag	-catch, -lamp, -net, -pin, valve
sago	ged, ging, s
said	s
sail* (travel by ship)	ed, ing, s
sailor	s
saint	s

∉ Drop e before adding ing

	rung	rung
	wrung	wrung

*	root	route
	route	rowed
	row	road
	roe	rode
	sail	
	sale	

sc

saintly	ier, iest, ily, iness
sake	s
salad	-dressing, -oil, s
salary	ies
sale *(selling)*	sman, smen, -room, s
salmon	**salmon**
saloon	s
salt	ed, ing, -water, -cellar, -spoon, s
salty	ier, iest, iness
salute	d, ting, s
salvage	d, ting, s
same	ness
sample	d, ting, r, s
sanatorium	s or **sanatoria**
sanctuary	ies
sand	-castle, -dune, paper, -storm, s
sandy	ier, iest, iness
sandal	s
sandwich	ed, ing, es

saucer	ful, s
saucy	ier, iest, ily, iness
saunter	ed, ing, s
sausage	-meat, -roll, s
savage	d, ting, ly, ry, ness, s
save	d, ting, s
saviour	s
saw	ed, ing, dust, mill, s
sawn or **sawed**	
Saxon	s
saxophone	s
say	ing, s
said	

sc

scabbard	s
scaffold	ing, s
scald	ed, ing, s

sang	
sank	
Santa Claus	
sap	ped, ping, ling, s
sapphire	s
sarcastic	ally
sardine	s
sash	es
satchel	s
satellite	s
satin	s
satisfaction	
satisfactory	ily, iness
satisfy	ing
satisfied	ies
saturate	d, e̸ing, s
Saturday	s
sauce	pan, s

scale	d, e̸ing, s
scalp	ed, ing, s
scamp	ed, ing, s
scamper	ed, ing, s
scan	ned, ning, ner, s
scar	red, ring, s
scarce	r, st, ly, ness
scarcity	ies
scare	d, e̸ing, r, crow, s
scarf	-ring, s or **scarves**
scarlet	s
scatter	ed, ing, -brain, s
scavenge	d, e̸ing, r, s
scene* (view; place)	-shifter, s
scenery	
scent* (smell; perfume)	ed, ing, s
scheme	d, e̸ing, r, s
scholar	ship, s

e̸ Drop e before adding ing

* sale
  sail

scene
seen

scent
sent

se

scholastic	ally
school	ed, ing, boy, girl, -teacher, s
schoolmaster	s
schoolmistress	es
schooner	s
science	-fiction, s
scientific	ally
scientist	s
scissors	**scissors**
scold	ed, ing, er, s
scone	s
scoop	ed, ing, er, s
scooter	s
scorch	ed, ing, es
score	d, éing, r, -board, -card, s
scorn	ed, ing, er, s
scornful	ly, ness
scorpion	s
scoundrel	s

scroll	s
scrub	bed, bing, ber, s
scrum	med, ming, mage, s
scuffle	d, éing, r, s
scull* (oar; to row)	ed, ing, er, s
scullery	ies
sculptor	s
sculptress	es
sculpture	d, éing, s
scuttle	d, éing, s
scythe	d, éing, s

se

sea*	side, sick, shore, front, port, s
sea*	-gull, -horse, -lion, -serpent, s
sea*	man, men, -shell, -water, weed, s
Sea Scout	s
seal	ed, ing, er, skin, s

scour	ed, ing, er, s
scout	ed, ing, er; master, s
scowl	ed, ing, er; s
scraggy	ier; iest, ily, iness
scramble	d, ✗ing, r; s
scrap	ped, ping, py, -book, -heap, s
scrape	d, ✗ing, r; s
scratch	ed, ing, es
scratchy	ier; iest, ily, iness
scrawl	ed, ing, er; s
scrawly	ier; iest, iness
scream	ed, ✗ing, er; s
screech	ed, ing, es
screechy	ier; iest, ily, iness
screen	ed, ing, s
screw	ed, ing, driver; s
scribble	d, ✗ing, r; s
scripture	s

sealing* (fastening)	-wax
seam* (join; rock vein)	less, s
search	ed, ing, es
searchlight	s
season	-ticket, s
seat	ed, ing, er, -belt, s
seclude	d, ✗ing, s
second	ly, -class, -hand, -rate, s
secondary	
secrecy	
secret	ive, ly, s
secretary	ies
section	ed, ing, s
secure	d, ✗ing, ly, ness, s
security	ies
see* (notice)	ing, s
seed	ed, ing, ✗, ling, -bed, -cake, s
seek	ing, er, s

✗ Drop e before adding ing

sealing	seam
ceiling	seem

scull	sea
skull	see

*

seem* (appear)	ed, ing, s
seen* (noticed)	
see-saw	ed, ing, s
seize	d, ϕing, s
seldom	
select	ed, ing, ion, s
self	–conscious, –service, **selves**
selfish	ly, ness
sell* (exchange for money)	ing, er,* s
sellotape	d, ϕing, s
semicircle	s
semicircular	ly
semi-detached	
semolina	
send	ing, er, s
senior	s
sensation	al, ally, s
sense	d, ϕing, s
senseless	ly, ness

servant	–girl, s
serve	d, ϕing, r, s
service	d, ϕing, s
serviette	s
session	s
set	ting, ter, –square, s
settee	s
settle	d, ϕing, r, ment, s
several	
severe	r, st, ly
severity	
sew* (stitch)	ed, ing, er, s
sewing-machine	s
sewn* (fastened with stitches)	
sextet(te)	s

shabby	ier, iest, ily, iness
shack	s

sensible	ness		**shade**	d, e̸ing, s
sensibly			**shady**	ier, iest, ily, iness
sent* (send)			**shadow**	ed, ing, s
sentence	d, e̸ing, s		**shadowy**	ily, iness
sentinel	s		**shaft**	s
sentry	ies		**shaggy**	ier, iest, ily, iness
separate	d, e̸ing, ly, ness, s		**shake**	n, e̸ing, r, s
separation	s		**shaky**	ier, iest, ily, iness
September			**shall**	
sequin	s		**shallow**	er, est, ly, ness, s
serenade	d, e̸ing, r, s		**shamble**	d, e̸ing, s
serf* (villein; slave)	dom, s		**shame**	d, e̸ing, s
sergeant	-major; s		**shameful**	ly, ness
serial* (in parts—as story or film)	s		**shameless**	ly, ness
series			**shampoo**	ed, ing, s
serious	ly, ness		**shamrock**	s
sermon	s		**shandy**	ies
serpent	s		**shan't** (shall not)	

*	seem	seen	sent	serf	serial	seller	sell	seen	seem	sew	sewn
	seam	scene	scent	surf	cereal	cellar	cell	scene		sow	sown
										so	

shanty	ies
shape	d, ding, ly, s
shapeless	ly, ness
share	d, ding, s
shark	skin, s
sharp	er, est, ly ness, -shooter, s
sharpen	ed, ing, er, s
shatter	ed, ing, s
shave	n, d, ding, r, s
shawl	s
sheaf	**sheaves**
shear* (cut; clip)	ed, ing, er, s
sheath	s
sheath-knife	-knives
shed	ding, der, s
sheep	-dog, -farmer, -pen, skin, **sheep**
sheer* (steep)	
sheet	s
sheik(h)	s

shipwreck	ed, ing, s
shirk	ed, ing, er, s
shirt	-button, -sleeve, -tail, s
shiver	ing, y, s
shoal	ed, ing, s
shock	ed, ing, s
shoddy	ier, iest, ily, iness
shoe*	ing, -bag, horn, -lace, maker, s
shod	
shone	
shoo* (frighten away)	ed, ing, s
shook	
shoot* (fire)	ing, er, s
shop	ped, ping, per, keeper; lifter, s
shore* (sea shore)	s
shorn	
short	age, er, est, ly, ness, bread, s
shorten	ed, ing, s
shorthand	

shelf	**shelves**	**shot**	-gun, s
shell	ed, ing, er; s	**should**	
shellfish	es or **shellfish**	**shouldn't** (should not)	
she'll (she will; she shall)		**shoulder**	ed, ing, -bag, -blade, -strap, s
shelter	ed, ing, s	**shout**	ed, ing, er; s
shepherd	s	**shovel**	led, ling, ler; s
shepherdess	es	**show**	n, ed, ing, -case, room, s
sherbet	s		-jumping, -ground, s
sheriff	s	**shower**	ed, ing, -bath; s
sherry	ies	**shower**y	ier; iest, iness
she's (she is; she has)		**shrank**	
shield	ed, ing, s	**shred**	ded, ding, der; s
shift	ed, ing, y, er; s	**shrewd**	er, est, ly, ness
shin	ned, ning, -guard, -pad, s	**shriek**	ed, ing, er; s
shine	d'ing, s	**shrill**	er, est, y, ness; s
shiny	ier, iest, ily, iness	**shrimp**	ed, ing, er, s or **shrimp**
shingle	s	**shrine**	s
ship	ped, ping, load, mate, yard, s	**shrink**	ing, able, age, s

é Drop e before adding ing

	shear	shoe	shoot	shore
*	sheer	shoo	chute	sure

shu shy si

shrivel	led, ling, s
shrub	s
shrubbery	ies
shrug	ged, ging, s
shrunk	en
shudder	ed, ⅆing, s
shuffle	d, ⅆing, r, s
shun	ned, ning, s
shunt	ed, ing, er, s
shut	ting, s
shutter	ed, ing, s
shuttle	d, ⅆing, cock, s
shy	er, est, ly, ness

si

sick	er, est, ly, ness, -bay, -bed, -room
sicken	ed, ing, s

silent	ly
silhouette	d, ⅆing, s
silk	en, worm, s
silky	ier, iest, ily, iness
silly	ier, iest, ily, iness, ies
silver	ed, ing, y, -paper, -plated
similar	ly
similarity	ies
simmer	ed, ing, s
simple	r, st, ness, ton, -minded
simplicity	
simply	
simplify	ication, ies
simplified	
simultaneous	ly, ness
sin	ned, ning, ner, s
since	
sincere	ly, ness
sincerity	r, st, ly, ness

side d, *é*ing, car, light, line, -show, s	**sing** ing, er, -song, s
sideboard s	**singe** d, ing, s
sideways	**single** d, *é*ing, *é*y, -handed, s
siege s	**singular** ly, s
sieve d, *é*ing, s	**sinister** ly
sift ed, ing, er, s	**sink** ing, er, s
sigh ed, ing, s	**sip** ped, ping, per, s
sight* (see) ed, ing, less, seeing, seer, s	**siphon** ed, ing, s
sign ed, ing, board, -writer, post, s	**sister** ly, s
signal led, ling, ler, man, men, s	**sister(s)-in-law**
signal-box es	**sit** ting, ter, s
signature -tune, s	**sitting-room** s
signet* (a seal) -ring, s	**site*** (a place) d, *é*ing, s
significance	**situated**
significant ly	**situation** s
signify ing	**size** d, *é*ing, s
signified ies	**sizzle** d, *é*ing, s
silence d, *é*ing, r, s	

é Drop **e** before adding *ing*

*	sight	signet
	site	cygnet

sk sl

sk

skate	d, -ing, r; board, s
skating-rink	s
skein	s
skeleton	s
sketch	ed, ing, es
sketchy	ier, iest, ily, iness
skewer	ed, ing, s
ski	-ed, -ing, er, -jump, -lift, -run, s
skid	ded, ding, s
skilful	ly, ness
skill	ed, s
skim	med, ming, mer, s
skin	ned, ning, -diving, -diver, s
skinny	ier, iest, iness
skip	ped, ping, per; s
skipping-rope	s
skipper	ed, ing, s
skirmish	ed, ing, es

sl

slate	s
slaughter	ed, ing, er, -house, s
slave	d, -ing, r; ry, -driver, -trader; s
slay* (kill)	ing, er; s
sledge	d, -ing, r; s
sleek	ed, ing, er, est, ly, ness, s
sleep	ing, er; less, -walking, -walker, s
sleepy	ier, iest, ily, iness
slept	
sleet	ier, iest, iness
sleety	
sleeve	d, less, -button, s
sleigh* (sledge)	ing, -bell, -horse, s
slender	ly, ness
sleuth	-hound, s
slew	
slice	d, -ing, r; s
slick	ed, ing, er, est, ly, ness, s
slid	

skirt	ed, ing, s		**slide**	ding, r; s
skittle	d, ding, r, -alley, -ball, -pin, s		**slight**	ed, ing, er, est, ly, ness, s
skull* (head bones)			**slim**	med, ming, mer; mest, ly, ness, s
skulk	-cap, s		**slime**	
skunk	ed, ing, s		**slimy**	ier; iest, ily, iness
sky	ing, lark, light, -rocket, scraper		**sling**	ing, er; s
skied	ies		**slink**	ing, er; s
			slinky	ier; iest, ily, iness
			slip	ped, ping, knot, shod, way; s
sl			**slipper**	s
			slippery	ier; iest, ily, iness
slack	ed, ing, er, est, ly, ness, s		**slit**	ting, ter; s
slacken	ed, ing, s		**slither**	ed, ing, y; s
slain			**sloe*** (wild plum)	-tree, s
slam	med, ming, s		**slog**	ged, ging, ger; s
slang	ing, y		**slogan**	s
slant	ed, ing, wise, s		**slop**	ped, ping, -basin, s
slap	ped, ping per, dash, stick, s		**sloppy**	ier; iest, ily, iness
slash	ed, ing, es			

ĕ Drop **e** before adding **ing**

skull	slay	sloe
scull	sleigh	slow
*		

sm

slope	d, *t*ing, s
slot	ted, ting, -machine, -meter, s
slouch	ed, ing, es
slovenly	ier, iest, iness
slow*	ed, ing, er, est, ly, ness, s
slow-worm	s
slug	s
sluggish	ly, ness
sluice	d, *t*ing, -gate, s
slum	my, -dweller, s
slumber	ed, ing, er, s
slump	ed, ing, s
slung	
slunk	
slush	ed, ing, es
slushy	ier, iest, ily, iness
sly	er, est, ly, ness

sn

smother	ed, ing, s
smoulder	ed, ing, s
smudge	d, *t*ing, s
smudgy	ier, iest, ily, iness
smuggle	d, ing, er, s
smut	ted, ting, s
smutty	ier, iest, ily, iness

sn

snack	-bar, s
snail	s
snake	d, *t*ing, *e*y, -bite, -charmer, s
snap	ped, ping, per, shot, dragon, s
snare	d, *t*ing, r, s
snarl	ed, ing, er, s
snatch	ed, ing, es
sneak	ed, ing, er, s
sneaky	ier, iest, ily, iness

sm

smack — ed, ing, s
small — er, est, ness
smart — ed, ing, er, est, ly, ness, s
smarten — ed, ing, s
smash — ed, ing, es
smear — ed, ing, s
smeary — ier, iest, ily, iness
smell — ed, ing, er, s
smelly — ier, iest, ily, iness
smelt or **smelled**
smile — d, e̶ing, r, s
smirk — ed, ing, er, s
smithereens
smock — ed, ing, s
smoke — d, e̶ing, r, -bomb, -screen, s
smoky — ier, iest, ily, iness
smooth — ed, ing, er, est, ly, ness, s

sneer — ed, ing, r, s
sneeze — d, ing, r, s
sniff — ed, ing, er, s
sniffle — d, e̶ing, r, s
snigger — ed, ing, er, s
snip — ped, ping, per, s
snipe — d, e̶ing, r, s
snivel — led, ling, ler, s
snob — bery, bish, bishness, s
snooker — ed
snore — d, e̶ing, r, s
snort — ed, ing, er, s
snow — ed, ing, drift, fall, -plough, drop, shoe, s
snowball — man, men, -storm, s
snowy — ier, iest, ily, iness
snug — ger, gest, ly, ness
snuggle — d, e̶ing, s

e̶ Drop **e** before adding **ing**

* slow
  sloe

so

soak	ed, ing, s
soap	ed, ing, -suds, -bubble, -flake, s
soapy	ier, iest, ily, iness
soar* (fly upwards)	ed, ing, s
sob	bed, bing, s
sociable	ness
social	ly, s
socialist	s
society	ies
sock	s
socket	s
soda	-bread, -fountain, -water
sodden	
sofa	s
soft	er, est, ish, ly, ness, -hearted
soften	ed, ing, er, s
soggy	ier, iest, ily, iness
soil	ed, ing, s

spa

soon	er, est
soot	
sooty	ier, iest, ily, iness
soothe	d, ing, s
soprano	s
sore* (painful)	r, st, ly, ness, s
sorrow	ed, ing, ful, fully, s
sorry	ier, iest, ily, iness
sort	ed, ing, er, s
soul* (spirit)	ful, fully, s
sound	ed, ing, er, est, ly, ness, s
soup	-plate, -spoon, s
sour	ed, ing, er, est, ly, ness, s
source	s
south	-east, -west, ern, erly, ward
souvenir	s
sovereign	s
sow* (scatter seed)	ed, ing, er, s
sown* (planted)	

sold* (sell)	ed, ing, s
solder	ed, ing, s
soldier	s
sole* (only)	ly
sole* (bottom of shoe, etc.)	d,* ing, s
sole* (fish)	s or **sole**
solemn	ity, ly, ness
solicitor	s
solid	ity, ly, s
solitary	ily
solo	ist, -singer; s
solution	s
solve	d, ing, s
some*	body, one, how, thing, where
sometime	s
somersault	ed, ing, s
son* (boy)	ny; s
song	ster; book, -bird, -writer; s

sp

space	d, ing, r, s, craft, man, men
space	-capsule, ship, -station, suit, s
spacious	ly, ness
spade	ful, s
spaghetti	
span	ned, ning, s
spangle	d, ing, s
spaniel	s
spank	ed, ing, s
spanner	s
spare	d, ing, s
spark	ed, ing, s
sparkle	d, ing, s
sparrow	-hawk, s
spastic	s

					é Drop *e* before adding *ing*
					sow	sown
					sew	sewn
					so

*	soar	sold	sole	some	son
	sore	soled	soul	sum	sun

spat
spawn ed, ing, s
speak ing, er, s
spear ed, ing, man, men, head, -gun, s
special ly, ty, ist, ity
specialize d, ∂ing, s
specimen s
speck ed, ing, less, lessly, s
speckle d, ∂ing, s
spectacle s
spectacular ly
spectator s
spectre s
sped or **speeded**
speech -training, less, es
speed ed, ing, -boat, -limit, way, s
speedy ier, iest, ily, iness
spell ed, ing, er, bind, bound, s
spelt or **spelled**

splash ed, ing, es
splendid ly
splendour s
splint s
splinter ed, ing, y, s
split ting, ter, s
splutter ed, ing, er, s
spoil ed, ing, er, -sport, s
spoilt or **spoiled**
spoke (speak) n, sman, smen
spoke (of wheel) s
sponge d, ∂ing, r, -bag, -cake, s
spongy ier, iest, ily, iness
spool s
spoon ed, ing, ful, s
sport ed, ing, sman, smen, s
sporty ier, iest, ily, iness
spot ted, ting, ter, less, lessly, light, s
spotty ier, iest, ily, iness

spend	ing, er, thrift, s		**spout**	ed, ing, s
spent			**sprain**	ed, ing, s
sphere	s		**sprang**	
spider	y, s		**sprat**	s or **sprat**
spied			**sprawl**	ed, ing, er, s
spike	d, *e*ing, s		**spray**	ed, ing, er, s
spill	ed, ing, s		**spread**	ing, er, s
spilt or **spilled**			**spring**	ing, -cleaning, -board, -time, s
spin	ning, ner, -dryer; s		**springy**	ier, iest, ily, iness
spinach			**sprinkle**	d, *e*ing, r, s
spinster	s		**sprint**	ed, ing, er; s
spiral	led, ling, ly, s		**sprout**	ed, ing, s
spire	s		**sprung**	
spirit	ed, ing, -level, -lamp, s		**spun**	
spirt or **spurt**	ting, ter; s		**spur**	red, ring, s
spit	d, *e*ing, s		**spurt** or **spirt**	ed, ing, s
spite	d, *e*ing, s		**spy**	ing
spiteful	ly, ness		**spied**	ies

é Drop **e** before adding **ing**

sq

squabble	d, éing, r, s
squad	ron, s
squall	ed, éing, y, s
squander	ed, ing, er; s
square	d, éing, ly, ness, -dance, root, s
squash	ed, ing, y, es
squat	ted, ting, ter; s
squaw	s
squawk	ed, ing, er; s
squeak	ed, ing, er; s
squeaky	ier, iest, ily, iness
squeal	ed, ing, er; s
squeeze	d, éing, r; s
squelch	ed, ing, es
squib	s
squint	ed, ing, er; s
squire	d, éing, s
squirm	ed, ing, er; s

ste

stalk	ed, ing, er; s
stall	ed, ing, -holder; s
stallion	s
stammer	ed, ing, er; s
stamp	ed, ing, -album, -collector; s
stampede	d, éing, s
stand	ing, s
standard	-bearer; s
star	red, ring, less, light, lit, s
starry	ier, iest, ily, iness
starboard	
starfish	es or **starfish**
starch	ed, ing, es
stare* (look at)	d, éing, s
starling	s
start	ed, ing, er; s
startle	d, éing, s
starvation	
starve	d, éing, s

squirrel	s
squirt	ed, ing, er, s

st

stab	bed, bing, ber, s
stable	d, éing, -man, -men, -boy, s
stack	ed, ing, s
stadium	s or **stadia**
staff	ed, ing, -room, s
stag	-beetle, -horn, hound, -hunt, s
stage	d, éing, -hand, -manager, s
stage-coach	es
stagger	ed, ing, er, s
stain	ed, ing, less, er, s
stair*	-carpet, case, -rod, way, s
stake* (a stick; bet)	d, éing, s
stale	r, st, ly, ness

state	d, éing, ment, s
stately	ier, iest, ily, iness
station	ed, ing, -master, s
stationary* (still)	s
stationer	
stationery* (paper, pens, etc.)	
statue	tte, s
staunch	ed, ing, er, est, ly, ness, es
stay	ed, ing, er, s
steady	ing
steadied	
steak* (meat)	ier, iest, ily, iness, ies
steal* (thieve)	s
stealth	
stealthy	ing, s
steam	ier, iest, ily, iness
steamy	ed, ing, er, boat, ship, -engine, s
steel* (metal)	ier, iest, ily, iness
	ed, ing, y, work, worker, s

é Drop e before adding ing

stair	stake	stationary	steal
stare	steak	stationery	steel
*			

steep	er, est, ly, ness
steeple	chase, jack, s
steer	age, ed, ing, er, sman, smen, s
steering-wheel	s
stem	med, ming, s
stencil	led, ling, ler, s
step	ped, ping, -ladder, s
step	father, mother, brother, sister, s
stepping-stone	s
sterilize	d, ∉ing, r, s
stern	er, est, ly, ness
stew	ed, ing, er, -pot, s
steward	s
stewardess	es
stick	ing, er, -insect, s
sticky	ier, iest, ily, iness
stickleback	s
stiff	er, est, ly, ness
stiffen	ed, ing, er, s

stool	-ball, s
stoop	ed, ing, s
stop	ped, ping, page, per, s
storage	
store	d, ∉ing, house, keeper, -room, s
storey* (floor)	s
stork	s
storm	ed, ing, -cloud, s
stormy	ier, iest, ily, iness
story* (tale; floor)	ies
stout	er, est, ly, ness, ish, hearted
stove	-pipe, s
stow	ed, ing, away, s
straggle	d, ∉ing, r, s
straight* (not bent)	er, est, ly, ness
straighten	ed, ing, er, s
strain	ed, ing, er, s
strait* (sea channel)	s
strand	ed, ing, s

stifle	d, *e*ing, r, s		**strange**	r, st, ly, ness
stile* (steps)	s		**stranger**	s
still	ed, ing, ness, s		**strangle**	d, *e*ing, hold, r, s
sting	ing, er, s		**strap**	ped, ping, less, s
stinging-nettle	s		**straw**	board, -coloured, -hat, s
stir	red, ring, rer, s		**strawberry**	ies
stirrup	s		**stray**	ed, ing, er; s
stitch	ed, ing, es		**streak**	ed, ing, er; s
stoat	s		**streaky**	ier; iest, ily, iness
stock	ed, ing, ist, -car, -pot, -room, s		**stream**	ed, ing, lined, er; s
stocking	s		**street**	-sweeper; s
stockade	d, *e*ing, s		**strength**	s
stoke	d, *e*ing, r, s		**strengthen**	ed, ing, er; s
stole	n		**strenuous**	ly, ness
stomach	-ache, -pump, s		**stretch**	ed, ing, es
stone	d, *e*ing, -cold, -deaf, -mason, s		**stretcher**	-bearer; s
stony	ier; iest, ily, iness		**strict**	er, est, ly, ness
stood			**stride**	*e*ing, r; s

e Drop e before adding ing

	stile	straight	
	style	strait	

*

strike	e(ing, r, s
string	ing, -bag, -vest, s
strip	ped, ping, per, -lighting, s
stripe	d, e(ing, s
strode	
stroke	d, e(ing, r, s
stroll	ed, ing, er, s
strong	er, est, ly, ish, hold, -room
struck	
structure	s
struggle	d, e(ing, r, s
strum	med, ming, mer; s
strung	
strut	ted, ting, ter; s
stub	bed, bing, by, s
stubborn	ly, ness
stuck	
stud	ded, ding, s
student	s

subject	ed, ing, s
submarine	r, s
submerge	d, e(ing, s
submit	ted, ting, s
subscribe	d, e(ing, r, s
subscription	s
subside	d, e(ing, s
substance	s
substantial	ly
substitute	d, e(ing, s
subtract	ed, ing, ion, s
suburb	s
succeed	ed, ing, s
success	es
successful	ly
succession	s
successor	s
such	like

studio	s
studious	ly, ness
study	ing
studied	ies
stuff	ed, ing, er, s
stuffy	ier, iest, ily, iness
stumble	d, ∉ing, r, s
stump	ed, ing, s
stumpy	ier, iest, ily, iness
stun	ned, ning, ner, s
stung	
stunt	ed, ing, man, men, s
stupendous	ly, ness
stupid	ity, ly
sturdy	ier, iest, ily, iness
stutter	ed, ing, er, s
sty	ies
style* (way; fashion)	d, ∉ing, s

suck	ed, ing, er, s
suction	
sudden	ly, ness
suds	
suet	-pudding, y
suffer	ed, ing, er, s
sufficient	ly
suffocate	d, ∉ing, s
suffocation	
sugar	ed, ing, y, -basin, -beet, -cane, s
suggest	ed, ing, ion, s
suicide	s
suit	ed, ing, able, ably, ability, case, s
suite* (set of furniture, rooms, etc.)	s
sulk	ed, ing, s
sulky	ier, iest, ily, iness
sullen	ly, ness
sultana	s

*
style	suite
stile	sweet

sum* (add up; total)	med, ming, s
summer	y, -time, -house, s
summit	s
summon	ed, ing, s
summons	es
sumptuous	ly, ness
sun* ned, ning, beam, light, flower, s	
sun* -glasses, rise, set, shine, shade, s	
sunny	ier, iest, ily, iness
sunbathe	d, ding, r, s
sunburn	ed, t
sundae* (ice cream)	s
Sunday*	-school, s
sung	
sunk	en
superb	ly
superintend	ed, ing, ent, s
superior	ity, s
supermarket	s

surplice* (gown)	s
surplus* (left over)	es
surprise	d, ďing, s
surrender	ed, ing, s
surround	ed, ing, s
survey	ed, ing, or, s
survival	
survive	d, ďing, s
survivor	s
suspect	ed, ing, s
suspend	ed, ing, er, s
suspense	
suspicion	s
suspicious	ly, ness
sustain	ed, ing, s

sw

swagger	ed, ing, er, -cane, -coat, -stick, s
swallow	ed, ing, er, s

superstition	
superstitious	ly, ness
supervise	d, éing, s
supervision	
supervisor	s
supper	-time, s
supple	ness
supply	ing
supplied	ier; ies
support	ed, ing, er; s
suppose	d, éing, s
sure* (certain)	r, st, ly, ness, -footed
surface	ing, -board, -riding
surge	d, éing, s
surgeon	s
surgery	ies
surname	s

swam	
swamp	s
swampy	ier; iest; ily, iness
swan	s
swap or **swop**	
swarm	ed, ing, s
swarthy	ier; iest; ily, iness
sway	ed, ing, s
swear	ing, er, -word, s
sweat	ed, ing, y, er; -band, -shirt, -suit, s
swede	s
sweep	ing, er, stake, s
swept	
sweet*	er, est, ish, ly, ness, heart, -pea, s
sweeten	ed, ing, er;
swell	ed, ing, s
swelter	ed, ing, s
swept	

é Drop e before adding ing

*						
sum	sun	sundae	sure	surf	sweet	surplice
some	son	Sunday	shore	serf	suite	surplus

swerve	d, d'ing, s
swift	er; est, ly, ness, s
swill	ed, ing, s
swim	mer, suit, s
swimming	-bath, -pool
swindle	d, d'ing, r, s
swine	herd, **swine**
swing	ing, er; s
swipe	d, d'ing, r, s
swirl	ed, ing, s
switch	ed, ing, es
swivel	ed, ing, es
swollen	led, ling, s
swoon	ed, ing, s
swoop	ed, ing, s
swop or **swap**	ped, ping, per, s
sword	sman, smen, -dance, s

tabby-cat	s
table	-tennis, -cloth, -mat, s
table-spoon	ful, s
tableau	x or s
tablet	s
tack	ed, ing, s
tackle	d, d'ing, r, s
tact	ful, fully, less, lessly
tactics	
tadpole	s
tag	ged, ging, s
tail*	ed, ing, -end, -lamp, -light, -spin, s
tailor	ed, ing, -made, s
take	n, d'ing, r, -away, -off, s
talcum powder	
tale* (story)	-bearer; -teller; s
talent	ed, s
talk	ative, ed, ing, er; s

swordfish	es or **swordfish**
swore	
sworn	
swum	
swung	

sy

sycamore	-tree, s
sympathetic	ally
sympathize	d, éing, r, s
sympathy	ies
symphony	ies
symptom	s
synagogue	s
syringe	d, éing, s
syrup	y
system	atic, atically, s

tall	er, est, ish, ness
tambourine	s
tame	d, éing, r, st, ly, ness, s
tamper	ed, ing, er, s
tan	ned, ning, ner, s
tandem	s
tangerine	s
tangle	d, éing, s
tango	d, éing, s
tank	ed, ing, s
tankard	er, ful, -trap, s
tantalize	d, éing, s
tantrum	s
tap	ped, ping, per, -dance, -dancing, s
tape	d, éing, s
tape	-measure, -recorder, -recording, s
tapestry	ies
tapioca	

é Drop **e** before adding **ing**

* tail
  tale

te

tar	red, ring, ry, s
tarantula	s
tare* (weed)	s
target	s
tarnish	ed, ing, es
tarpaulin	s
tart	let, s
tartan	s
task	ed, ing, master, s
tassel	s
taste	d, ∉ing, r, s
tasteful	ly, ness
tasteless	ly, ness
tatter	ed, ing, s
tattoo	ed, ing, er, ist, -mark, s
taught* (teach)	
taunt	ed, ing, er, s
taut* (tight)	er, est, ly, ness
tavern	s

tease	d, ∉ing, r, s
technical	ly
technician	s
Teddy bear	s
tedious	ly, ness
tee* (golf)	d, ing, -shot, s
tee-shirt or **T-shirt**	
teem* (pour; swarm)	s
teenage	ed, ing, s
teenager	s
teeth	d, -boy, -girl
telegram	s
telegraph	ed, ing, -line, -pole, -wire, s
telephone	d, ∉ing, s
telescope	d, ∉ing, s
televise	d, ∉ing, s
television	s
tell	ing, er, -tale, s
temper	ed, ing, s

tax	ation, ed, ing, es
taxi	-cab, -driver, -rank, s

te

tea*	cake, -cloth, cup, pot, -service, s
tea*	-set, -things, -time, -table, -tray, s
tea-cosy	ies
tea-leaf	-leaves
tea-party	ies
tea-spoon	ful, s
teach	ing, ings, es
teacher	s
teak	
team* (side; number)	-work, s
tear* (pull apart)	ing, s
tear	-gas, -drop, s
tearful	ly, ness

temperature	s
temple	s
temporary	ily
tempt	ation, ed, ing, er, s
tend	ed, ing, s
tender	-hearted, ly ness
tenement	s
tennis	-ball, -court, -racket
tenor	s
tense	d, e̸ing, r, st, ly, ness, s
tent	-peg, -pole, -rope, s
tentacle	s
tepid	ly, ness
term	ly, ed, ing, s
terminus	es or **termini**
terrace	d, e̸ing, -house, s
terrible	ness
terribly	

---

			e̸ Drop e before adding *ing*
		tea	team
		tee	teem
*	tare	taught	
	tear	taut	

th

terrier s
terrific ally
terrify ing
terrified ies
territorial s
territory ies
terror ism, ist, -stricken, s
terrorize d, ♦ing, s
test ed, ing, -paper, -piece, -tube, s
testament s
testimonial s
tetanus s
tether ed, ing, s
text -book, s
textile s

th

than
thank ed, ing, -offering, s

thermos flask s
these
they
they'll (they will; they shall)
they're* (they are)
they've (they have)
thick er, est, ly, ness, ish, -skinned
thicken ed, ing, er, s
thicket s
thief thieves
thieve d, ♦ing, s
thimble s
thin ned, ning, ner, nest, ly, ness, s
thing s
think ing, er, s
thirst ed, ing, s
thirsty ier, iest, ily, iness
this
thistle s

thankful	ly, ness
thankless	ly, ness
that	
that's (that is)	
thatch	ed, ing, es
thaw	ed, ing, s
theatre	-ticket, s
theatrical	ly, s
theft	
their* (belonging to them)	
theirs* (belonging to them)	
them	selves
then	
theory	ies
there* (in that place)	abouts, after
therefore	
there's (there is)	
thermometer	s

thorn	s
thorny	ier, iest, ily, iness
thorough	ly, ness, bred, fare
those	
though	
thought	s
thoughtful	ly, ness
thoughtless	ly, ness
thrash	ed, ing, ings, es
thread	ed, ing, bare, er, s
threat	s
threaten	ed, ing, s
thresh	ed, ing, es
threw* (throw)	
thrift	less
thrifty	ier, iest, ily, iness
thrill	ed, ing, er, s
thrive	d, ing, s

their	theirs
there	there's
they're	
*	

threw
through

ti | **to**

throat	
throb	bed, bing, s
throne* (king's seat)	s
throng	s
throttle	ed, ing, s
through* (from end to end)	out
throw	ing, er, n,* s
thrush	es
thrust	ing, s
thud	ded, ding, s
thug	s
thumb	ed, ing, -mark, -nail, screw, s
thump	ed, ing, er, s
thunder	ed, ing, y, bolt, clap, storm, s
Thursday	s

ti

tiara	s
tick	ed, ing, s

time	d, d/ing, r, ly, less, -bomb, table, s
timid	ity, ly, ness
tin	ned, ning, ny, -opener; foil, -tack, s
tinge	d, d/ing, s
tingle	d, d/ing, s
tinker	ed, ing, s
tinkle	d, d/ing, s
tinsel	led, ling, ly
tint	ed, ing, s
tiny	ier; iest, ily, iness
tip	ped, ping, per, ster, s
tiptoe	d, ing, s
tire* (weary)	d, d/ing, some, s
tired	ness
tireless	ly, ness
tissue	-paper, s
title	d, s
titter	ed, ing, s

ticket	-collector, -office, s		
tickle	d, ¢ing, r, s	**to*** (towards)	
ticklish	ly, ness	**toad**	-in-the-hole, s
tide* (sea)	-mark, s	**toadstool**	s
tidings		**to and fro**	
tidy	ing	**toast**	ed, ing, er, -rack, s
tidied	ier, iest, ily, iness, ies	**tobacco**	nist, -pipe, -plant, s
tie	d, *-clip, -pin, s	**toboggan**	ed, ing, er, s
tying		**today** or **to-day**	
tiger	-cat, -moth, s	**toddle**	d, ¢ing, r, s
tigress	es	**toe***	d, ing, -cap, -hold, -nail, s
tight	er, est, ly, ness, -rope, s	**toffee**	-apple, s
tighten	ed, ing, er, s	**together**	ness
tile	d, ¢ing, r, s	**toil**	ed, ing, er, s
till or **until**	ed, ing, er, s	**toilet**	-paper, -roll, -soap, s
tilt	ed, ing, er, s	**token**	s
timber	ed, -mill, -yard, s	**told**	

					¢ Drop e before adding *ing*
throne	through	tide	tire	toe	to
thrown	threw	tied	tyre	tow	too
					two (2)

*

tolerate d, d/ing, s
toll ed, ing, -bridge, -gate, s
tomahawk s
tomato es
tomb stone, s
tomcat s
tomorrow or **to-morrow** s
tomtit s
ton or **tonne** (metric) s
tone d, d/ing, -deaf, s
tongs s
tongue -tied, -twister, s
tonic s
tonight or **to-night** s
tonsil s
tonsillitis
too* (more than enough; also)
took
tool -bag, -chest, -shed, s

totter ed, ing, y, er, s
touch ed, ing, y, es
tough er, est, ly, ness, s
toughen ed, ing, s
tour ed, ing, ist, s
tournament s
tousle d, d/ing, s
tow* (pull) ed, ing, -line, -path, -rope, s
towards or **toward**
towel led, ling, -rail, s
tower ed, ing, -block, s
town -council, -crier, -hall, s
toy ed, ing, shop, s

tr

trace d, d/ing, r, s
tracing-paper

tooth	ache, paste, powder; less, **teeth**
tooth-brush	es
top	ped, ping, per, knot, -heavy, -hat, s
topic	s
topple	d, éing, s
topsy-turvy	
torch	es
tore	
torment	ed, ing, or, s
torn	
tornado	es
torpedo	ed, ing, es
torrent	s
torrential	ly
tortoise	-shell, s
torture	d, éing, r, -chamber, s
toss	ed, ing, es
total	led, ling, ly, s

track	ed, ing, er, suit, s
tractor	s
trade	d, éing, mark, sman, smen, r, s
traffic	-sign, -signal, -lights
tragedy	ies
tragic	ally
trail	ed, ing, er, s
train	ed, ing, er, s
traitor	ous, ously, s
tramp	ed, ing, er, s
trample	d, éing, r, s
trampoline	
transfer	red, ring, able, s
transform	ed, ing, ation, s
transistor	-radio, s
translate	d, éing, s
translation	

é Drop e before adding ing

	too	tow
	to	toe
*	two (2)	

transparent ly, ness
transport ed, ing, er, ation, able, s
trap ped, ping, per, -door, s
trapeze s
travel led, ling, ler, s
trawl ed, ing, er, s
tray -cloth, ful, s
treacherous ly, ness
treachery ies
treacle
tread ing, s
treason able
treasure d, ɗing, r, -chest, -hunt, s
treat ed, ing, ment, s
treble d, ɗing, s
tree -stump, -top, -trunk, s
trek ked, king, ker, s
trellis -work
tremble d, ɗing, s

trim med, ming, mer, mest, ly, ness, s
trinket s
trio s
trip ped, ping, per, s
triple d, ɗing, s
triplet s
tripod s
triumph ed, ing, ant, antly, s
trod den
trolley s
trombone ɗist, s
troop* (of scouts, soldiers) ed, ing, er, s
trophy ies
tropic al, ally, s
trot ted, ting, ter, s
trouble d, ɗing, some, -maker, s
trough s
troupe* (of entertainers) r, s
trousers

tremendous	ly, ness
trench	es
trespass	ed, ing, es
trespasser	s
trestle	-table, s
trial	s
triangle	s
tribe	sman, smen, s
tributary	ies
trick	ed, ing, ery, ster, s
tricky	ier, iest, ily, iness
trickle	d, éing, s
tricycle	d, éing, s
tried	
trier	s
tries	
trifle	d, éing, s
trigger	ed, ing, s

trousseau	x or s
trout	**trout**
trowel	s
truant	s
truck	-load, s
trudge	d, éing, s
true	r, st, ness
truly	
trumpet	ed, ing, er; -call, s
truncheon	s
trunk	ed, ing, es
truss	ed, ing, es
trust	ed, ing, worthy, s
trusty	ier, iest, ily, iness
truth	s
truthful	ly, ness
try	ing
tried	ier, ies

é Drop e before adding *ing*

troop
troupe
*

tu

tuba	
tubby	ier, iest, iness
tube	ed, ing, -train, s
tuck	ed, ing, -shop, s
Tudor	s
Tuesday	s
tuft	s
tug	ged, ging, ger, boat, s
tug-of-war	
tuition	s
tulip	s
tumble	d, ťing, r, down, -dryer, s
tumbler	s
tumult	ful, s
tumultuous	ly, ness
tundra	s
tune	d, ťing, r, s
tuneful	ly, ness

tw

twang	ed, ing, s
tweed	s
tweezers	
twice	
twiddle	d, ťing, r, s
twig	s
twilight	
twin	ned, ning, -brother, -sister, s
twine	d, ťing, s
twinge	d, ťing, s
twinkle	d, ťing, s
twirl	ed, ing, s
twist	ed, ing, er, s
twisty	ier, iest, ily, iness
twitch	ed, ing, es
twitter	ed, ing, s

tuneless	ly, ness
tunic	s
tunnel	led, ling, ler, s
turban	s
turbine	s
turf	ed, ing, s or **turves**
turkey	cock, s
Turkish delight	
turmoil	
turn	ed, ing, er, over, stile, table, s
turnip	s
turpentine	
turquoise	s
turret	ed, s
turtle	-neck, -shell, -soup, -dove, s
tusk	s
tussle	d, éing, s
tutor	ial, s

ty

tying	
type	d, éing, written, writing, writer, s
typist	s
typhoon	s
typical	ly, ness
tyrannize	d, éing, s
tyrant	s
tyre* (wheel cover)	s

ug

ugly	ier, iest, ily, iness

um

umbrella	-stand, s
umpire	d, éing, s

* tyre
   tire

é Drop e before adding *ing*

un

un

unable	
unafraid	
unaided	
unarm	ed, ing, s
unattractive	ly, ness
unavoidable	y
unaware	s
unbalance	d, ing, s
unbearable	y
unbeaten	
unbolt	ed, ing, s
unbuckle	d, ing, s
unbutton	ed, ing, s
uncanny	ily, iness
uncertain	ly, ty
uncivilized	
uncle	s
unclean	liness

undertake	n, ing, r, s
undertook	
undid	
undo	ing
undone	
undoubted	ly
undress	ed, ing, es
uneasy	ier, iest, ily, iness
unemployed	ment
uneven	ly, ness
unexpected	ly, ness
unexplored	
unfair	ly, ness
unfasten	ed, ing, s
unfinished	
unfit	ted, ting, s
unfold	ed, ing, s
unfortunate	ly
unfriendly	iness

uncomfortable	ness
uncommon	ly, ness
unconscious	ly, ness
uncork	ed, ing, s
uncover	ed, ing, s
uncurl	ed, ing, s
undamaged	
undecided	ly
under	clothes, clothing, wear
under	go, going, goes, gone, went
undercurrent	s
underground	
undergrowth	
underneath	
understand	able, ing, s
understood	
understudy	ing
understudied	ies

unfurnished	
ungrateful	ly, ness
unguarded	ly, ness
unhappy	ier, iest, ily, iness
unharmed	
unhealthy	ier, iest, ily, iness
unhurt	
uniform	ed, s
unimportant	
uninhabited	
uninjured	
uninteresting	
Union Jack	
unite	d, éing, s
universe	
university	ies
unjust	ly, ness
unkind	er, est, ly, ness

é Drop e before adding ing

up ur us

			up	
upbringing				s
upheaval				
upholster				ed, ing, er, s
upholstery				ies
upkeep				
upon				
upper				most, -cut, s
upright				ly, ness, s
uprising				s
uproar				s
uproot				ed, ing, s
upset				ing, s
upside-down				
upstairs				
upstream				
upturn				ed, ing, s
upward				ly, s

unknown	
unlawful	ly, ness
unless	
unlike	ness
unlikely	ier, iest, ihood
unload	ed, ing, s
unlock	ed, ing, s
unlucky	ier, iest, ily, iness
unmistakable	y
unnecessary	ily
unoccupied	
unpack	ed, ing, s
unpleasant	ly, ness
unpopular	ity, ly
unravel	led, lling, s
unreasonable	y
unreliable	ness
unroll	ed, ing, s
unsaddle	d, d'ing, s

unsafe	r, st, ly, ness
unscrew	ed, ing, s
unselfish	ly, ness
unsteady	ier, iest, ily, iness
unsuitable	
untangle	d, éing, s
untidy	ier, iest, ily, iness
untie	d, s
untying	
until or till	
untrue	
unusual	ly, ness
unveil	ed, ing, s
unwelcome	
unwell	
unwilling	ly, ness
unwise	ly
unwrap	ped, ping, s

ur

uranium	s
urban	
urchin	s
urge	d, éing, s
urgency	ies
urgent	ly
urn* (vase; tea-urn)	s

us

use	d, éing, r, s
useful	ly, ness
useless	ly, ness
usher	ed, ing, s
usherette	s
usual	ly, ness

* um
  earn

é Drop e before adding ing

ut va

ut

utensil	s
utmost	
utter	ed, ing, ance, s
utter	ly, most, ness

va

vacancy	ies
vacant	ly
vacate	d, éing, s
vacation	s
vaccinate	d, éing, s
vacuum	-cleaner, -flask, s
vague	r, st, ly, ness
vain* (proud)	
vale* (valley)	s
valentine	s
valiant	ly

ve

ve

veal	
vegetable	s
vegetarian	s
vegetation	
vehicle	s
veil* (a covering)	ed, ing, s
vein* (blood-vessel)	ed, ing, s
velvet	y, s
vengeance	
venison	
vent	ed, ing, -hole, s
ventilate	d, éing, s
ventilation	
ventilator	s
ventriloquist	s
venture	d, éing, some, s
veranda(h)	s
verb	al, ally, s

valley	s		**verdict**	s
valuable	s		**verge**	d, éing, s
value	d, éing, less, r, s		**verger**	s
valve	s		**vermilion**	s
vane* (weathercock)	s		**vermin**	ous, ously
vanilla			**verse**	s
vanish	ed, ing, es		**version**	s
vanity	ies		**versus**	
vanquish	ed, ing, es		**vertical**	ly
variety	ies		**very**	
various	ly, ness		**vessel**	s
varnish	ed, ing, es		**vest**	ed, ing, s
vary			**vestibule**	s
varied	ies		**vestry**	ies
vase	s		**vet**	ted, ting, s
vaseline			**veteran**	s
vast	er, est, ly, ness		**veterinary**	ies
vault	ed, ing, er, s		**vex**	ed, ing, es, ation, atious

é Drop **e** before adding **ing**

*	vain	vale
	vane	veil
	vein	

vi

viaduct	s
vibrate	d, &ing, s
vibration	s
vicar	age, s
vice	-admirable, -captain, s
vicious	ly, ness
victim	s
victor	s
victorious	ly, ness
victory	ies
victual	led, ling, ler; s
videotape	d, &ing, s
view	ed, ing, er, point, s
vigorous	ly, ness
vigour	
viking	s
vile	r, st, ly, ness
villa	s

vo

vocabulary	ies
vocalist	s
voice	d, &ing, s
volcano	es
vole	s
volley	ed, ing, -ball, s
volt	age, s
volume	s
voluntary	ily
volunteer	ed, ing, s
vomit	ed, ing, s
vote	d, &ing, r, s
vouch	ed, ing, es
voucher	s
vow	ed, ing, s
vowel	s
voyage	d, &ing, r, s

village		vulgar		ity, ly
villain* (scoundrel)	ous, ously, s	vulnerable		ness
villein* (serf)	s	vulture		s
vine	yard, s			
vinegar	y		**vu**	
violence				
violent	ly			
violet	s	**wa**		
violin	ist, s	waddle	d, *e*ing, r, s	
virtue	s	wade	d, *e*ing, r, s	
visible	y	wafer	s	
visibility		waft	ed, ing, er, s	
vision	s	wag	ged, ging, ger, s	
visit	ed, ing, or, s	wage	d, *e*ing, r, -earner, s	
vital	ity, ly	waggle	d, *e*ing, r, s	
vivaria	s or **vivaria**	wagon or **waggon**	er, -load, s	
vivarium	s or **vivaria**	waif	s	
vivid	ly, ness	wail	ed, ing, er, s	
vixen	s			

e Drop **e** before adding **ing**

villain
villein

*

we

waist* (of body)	coat, s
wait* (stay; serve)	ed, ing, s
waiter	s
waitress	es
waiting-room	s
wake	d, ɖing, r, s
waken	ed, ing, er, s
walk	ed, ing, er, s
walking-stick	s
wall	ed, ing, chart, flower, paper, s
wallet	s
wallow	ed, ing, er, s
walnut	-tree, s
walrus	es
waltz	ed, ing, es
wand	s
wander	ed, ing, er, s
wangle	d, ɖing, r, s
want	ed, ing, s

waste*	d, ɖing, land, -bin, -paper, -pipe, s
wasteful	ly, ness
watch	ed, ing, man, men, es
watchful	ly, ness
water	ed, ing, -colour, cress, fall, proof, s
water-lily	ies
watery	ier, iest, ily, iness
wave	d, ɖing, s
waver	ed, ing, er, s
wavy	ier, iest, ily, iness
wax	ed, ing, en, es, works
waxy	ier, iest, ily, iness
way* (direction; manner; road)	lay, side, s

we

weak* (not strong)	er, est, ly, ness, -kneed
weaken	ed, ing, s
weakling	s

war*	-dance, -paint, -path, ship, s
war-cry	ies
warrior	s
warble	d, *ing, r, s
ward	ed, ing, en, er, s
wardrobe	s
ware* (goods)	house, s
warm	th, ed, ing, er; est, ish, ly, s
warn* (be careful)	ed, ing, er; s
warp	ed, ing, s
warrant	ed, ing, s
warren	s
wart	s
wary	ier; iest, ily, iness
wash	able, ed, ing, es
washer	s
wasn't (was not)	
wasp	s

wealth	
wealthy	ier; iest, ily, iness
weapon	s
wear* (dressed in)	ing, er; s
weary	ing
wearied	ier; iest, ily, iness, ies
weasel	s
weather*	ed, ing, cock, -forecast, -vane, s
weave	d, *ing, r; s
we'd (we had; we should; we would)	
wed	ded, ding, s
wedding	-cake, -card, -day, -ring, -bell, s
wedding-dress	es
wedge	d, *ing, s
Wednesday	s
weed	ed, ing, er; -killer, s
weedy	ier; iest, iness
week* (seven days)	-day, -end, s

é Drop e before adding ing

*								
	waist	wait	war	ware	warm	way	weak	weather
	waste	weight	wore	wear	worn	weigh	week	whether

wh

weekly	ies
weep	ing, y, er, s
wept	
weigh* (measure heaviness)	ed, ing, s
weight* (heaviness)	ed, ing, -lifter, s
weighty	ier, iest, ily, iness
weir	s
weird	er, est, ly, ness
welcome	d, ing, s
weld	ed, ing, er, s
welfare	
well	-behaved, -bred, -wisher; s
we'll (we shall; we will)	
wellington boot	s
went	
wept	
we're (we are)	
were	
weren't (were not)	

where	abouts, as, by, fore, upon
wherever	
whether* (if)	ever
which* (what one? who?)	
whiff	ed, ing, s
while	d, *é*ing, s
whilst	
whimper	ed, ing, er, s
whine* (cry; wail)	d, *é*ing, r, s
whip	ped, ping, per, s
whippet	s
whirl	ed, ing, igig, pool, wind, s
whisk	ed, ing, er, s
whisker	ed, y, s
whisky	ies
whisper	ed, ing, er, s
whist	-drive
whistle	d, *é*ing, r, s
white	r, st, ly, ness, s

wh

west	em, erly, ward, wards
wet	ted, ting, ter, test, ly, ness, s
we've (we have)	

wh

whack	ed, ing, s
whale	≠ing, r, bone, -boat, s
wharf	s or **wharves**
what	ever, soever
what's (what is)	
wheat	-field, -flour, germ, s
wheedle	d, ≠ing, r, s
wheel	ed, ing, er, barrow, -chair, s
wheeze	d, ≠ing, s
whelk	s
when	ever
whence	

whiten	ed, ing, er, s
whitewash	ed, ing, es
whiting	s
Whit Sunday	
Whitsun	tide
whiz zes or **whizz**	ed, ing, es
who	ever
who'd (who had; who would)	
who'll (who will; who shall)	
who're (who are)	
who's* (who is)	
whom	soever
whole* (all; complete)	sale, some
wholly* (completely)	
whoop	
whortleberry	ed, ing, s
whose* (belonging to whom)	ies
why	

weigh	weight	whether	which
way	wait	weather	witch

*

≠ Drop e before adding *ing*

whine	whole	wholly
wine	hole	holy

wi

wicked	er, est, ly, ness
wicker	work
wicket	-keeper; s
wide	r, st, ly, spread, s
widen	ed, ing, er, s
width	ed, ing, er; s
widow	ed, ing, er; s
wield	ly, **wives**
wife	d, ing, r, s
wiggle	
wigwam	er, est, ly, ness, life, fowl, fire, s
wild	es
wilderness	ly, ness
wilful	ed, ing, -power, s
will	ly, ness
willing	-herb, -tree, -warbler, s
willow	ier, iest, ily, iness
wily	

wo

wise	r; st, ly
wish	ed, ing, es
wishful	ly, ness
wistful	ly, ness
wit	ted, less, s
witty	ier, iest, ily, iness
witch* (old woman)	ed, craft, -hunt
with	in, out
withdraw	al, ing, n, s
withdrew	
withstand	ed, ing, s
wither	ing, s
withstood	
witness	ed, ing, -box, es
wizard	ry; s
wizened	

wo

wobble	d, ing, r, s

win	ning, ner, s
wince	d, cing, s
wind (turn; twist)	ing, er, s
wind	ed, ing, -chart, fall, mill, ward, s
windy	ier, iest, ily, iness
windscreen	-cleaner, -ledge, -pane, -sill, s
wine* (a drink)	-wiper, s
wing	d, ing, er, -span, s
wink	ed, ing, er, s
winkle	d, cing, s
winter	ed, ing, -time, s
wintry	ier, iest, ily, iness
wipe	d, cing, r, s
wire	d, cing, -netting, -rope, -cutter, s
wireless	ed, ing, es
wiry	ier, iest, ily, iness
wisdom	-tooth, -teeth

woe	begone, s
woeful	ly, ness
woke	n
wolf	-cub, -pack, **wolves**
woman	hood, ly, **women**
won* (win)	
wonder	ed, ing, ment, land, s
wonderful	ly, ness
won't (will not)	
wood*	ed, man, men, -cutter, land, s
wooden	
wood-louse	-lice
woodpecker	s
woodwork	
wool	
woollen	s
woolly	ier, iest, ily, iness
word	ed, ing, s

é Drop e before adding *ing*

	won	wood
	one (I)	would

*
wine	witch
whine	which

wr

wore* (wear)	
work	ed, ing, man, men, shop, er, s
world	
worm	-famous, -wide, s
worm* (wear)	ed, ing, y, eaten, -cast, -hole, s
worried	-out
worry	ing
	ier, ies, isome
worse	
worsen	ed, ing, s
worst	
worship	ped, ping, per; s
worth	while
worthless	ly, ness
worthy	ier, iest, ily, iness, ies
would* (past of will)	
wouldn't (would not)	
wound (turned; twisted)	ed, ing, s
wound (injure)	n
wove	

x ya ye yi

writhe	d, d̶ing, s
wrong	ed, ing, ful, ly, ness, s
wrote	
wrung* (twisted)	
wry	er, est, ly, ness

x

X-ray	ed, ing, s
xylophone	s

ya

yacht	ing, sman, smen, -club, s
yak	s
yap	ped, ping, per; s
yard	age, stick, s
yarn	ed, ing, s
yawn	ed, ing, s

wr

wrangle	d, éing, r, s
wrap* (cover)	ped, ping, per, s
wrath	ful, fully
wreath	s
wreck	age, ed, ing, er, s
wren	s
wrestle	ed, ing, es
	d, éing, r, s
wretch	es
wretched	ly, ness
wriggle	d, éing, r, s
wring* (twist)	ing, er, s
wrinkle	d, éing, r, s
wrist	let, band, s
write* (form letters)	r, s
writing	-case, -desk, -paper, -table, s
written	

ye

year	ly, ling, s
yearn	ed, ing, s
yeast	y
yell	ed, ing, er, s
yellow	er, est, ness, ish, y, s
yelp	ed, ing, er, s
yeoman	men
yes	es
yesterday	s
yet	
yeti	s
yew*	-tree, s

yi

yield	ed, ing, s

é Drop e before adding ing

wore	worn	would	wring	write	wrung	yew
war	warn	wood	ring	right	rung	you
						ewe

*

yo yu ze   zi zo zu

	zi	
zigzag		ged, ging, s
zinc		
zip		ped, ping, per, -fastener, s
zither		s

	zo	
zodiac		
zone		d, ging, s
zoo		s
zoological garden		s
zoologist		s
zoology		
zoom		ed, ing, s

	zu	
Zulu		s

	yo	
yodel		led, ling, ler, s
yoga		
yog(h)urt		
yoke* (wooden bar; join)		d, ging, s
yokel		s
yolk* (of egg)		s
yonder		
Yorkshire pudding		s
you* (person)		s
you'd (you had; you would)		
you'll (you will)		
you're (you are)		
you've (you have)		
young		er, est, ish
youngster		s
your		
yours		
yourself		selves

youth		-club, s
youthful		ly, ness
yowl		ed, ing, er, s

yu

| yule | | -log, tide, s |

ze

zeal		ly
zealous		s
zebra		s
zebu		s
zephyr		s
zero		s
zest		ful, fully

¢ Drop **e** before adding **ing**

	you
	yew
	ewe

| yoke | |
| yolk | |

*

108

Parts of Speech

Noun

A naming word, e.g. *boy, man, cat, house, Susan, England*. On Monday John went by coach to *London Zoo* with his *teacher, Mr. Smith*, and other *children* from his *class*.

Pronoun

A word used instead of a noun, e.g. *me, she, it, we, us, him*. *You* and *I* will go now and *he* can come later with *them*.

Adjective

A word that is 'added to' a noun to describe it, e.g. *fat, thin, big, brown, green, ugly, pretty, delicious*. A *funny, little old* man with a *large* nose and a *grey* beard showed the *small* children his *beautiful* garden.

Verb

A doing word; a word that tells what is done, e.g. *do, go, stay, talk, shout, jump, lift, fight, eat, drink* Stop *running* or you will *fall* and *hurt* yourself.

Adverb

A word that tells how, when or where something happens, e.g. *soon, often, there, now, never, quickly, carefully, carelessly*. *Yesterday* when I came *here* I jumped *over* that wall.

Preposition   A word that is placed before a noun, e.g. *by, in, into, at, for, under, over, against, near*. Bob went with his sister on a bus to the town.

Conjunction   A word that joins sentences, phrases or words, e.g. *or, than, though, although, because, while, unless*. John and Mary will go if it is fine but not if it rains.

Interjection A word used as an exclamation, e.g. *Ah! Alas! Hey! Oh!* You did frighten me. *Ouch!* That hurt.

Article   One of the three words – *a, an* or *the*. A boy rode on an elephant at the zoo.

109

Spelling Lists of Words to Learn

The following lists contain the words you will need to use most often in your writing and compositions. You should, therefore, learn and try to remember how to spell all these words. Choose the shortest and easiest words at the beginning of each section to learn first. It is better to learn a few words each day rather than a long list, at one time, once a week. To make it easier for you the words are usually arranged in lists according to the number of letters in the words: three, four, five letters, etc. The number at the top of a word list shows the number of letters in each word in that list. Before you start to learn a list of words first study all the words in the list and notice that some words have the same order as others in the list.

All the words on pages 110 to 115 and at the bottom of page 118 are verbs, or may be used as verbs; and are arranged in lists according to the way in which their ed, ing, s endings are formed. When your teacher tests you on the words you have learnt he/she will probably ask you to spell some of these words with their ed, ing, s endings to see whether you have understood this, e.g.

bark
marked
parking
works

scare
scored
storing
stones

drop
chopped
shopping
stops

110

You may add ed, ing, s to all the following words, e.g.
camp ed, ing, s = **camped, camping, camps**

3	ed, ing, s	4	ed, ing, s	3	ed, ing, s	4	ed, ing, s
act		book		back		camp	
add		cook		pack		damp	
air		hook		sack		bump	
arm		look		dock		dump	
ask		cool		lock		jump	
end		pool		rock		lump	
ink		show		kick		pump	
oil		slow		lick		bomb	
own		flow		pick		comb	
toy		snow		tick		lamb	

4	ed, ing, s	4	ed, ing, s			4	ed, ing, s
dust		call				load	
last		fell				boat	
list		well				coat	

nest	yell	work	roar
rest	fill	cork	soap
test	kill	fork	help
post	mill	milk	long
lift	will	talk	hunt
melt	pull	walk	want
salt	roll	bank	word

4	4	4	4
form	gain	head	bath
farm	pain	heal	down
harm	rain	heat	even
warm	pair	seat	open
band	fail	fear	turn
hand	jail	near	join
land	nail	team	iron
sand	sail	play	part
bang	tail	pray	mind
gang	wait	stay	view

ed, ing, s   ed, ing, s   ed, ing, s   ed, ing, s

5 ed, ing, s	5 ed, ing, s	5 ed, ing, s	6 ed, ing, s
clean	knock	thank	answer
clear	clock	train	corner
climb	block	tramp	flower
cloud	shock	treat	bother
clown	black	light	gather
chain	crack	right	matter
chair	track	sight	master
chalk	brick	dream	murder
cheer	trick	radio	number
cheat	wreck	visit	wonder

5 ed, ing, s	5 ed, ing, s	6 ed, ing, s	6 ed, ing, s
enter	count	appear	remind
cover	cough	arrest	return
lower	rough	attack	reward
offer	round	happen	school
order	pound	hollow	scream
water	sound	follow	stream

paper
paint
point
plant

mouth
group
scout
shout

borrow
button
butter
letter

belong
poison
powder
obtain

5 — ed, ing, s
laugh
haunt
field
float
floor
flood
bloom
stoop
spoon
sport

5 — ed, ing, s
boast
coast
roast
toast
start
stamp
storm
allow
enjoy
guard

6 — ed, ing, s
colour
doctor
ground
garden
awaken
fasten
listen
pocket
rocket
ticket

7 — ed, ing, s
explain
contain
curtain
captain
holiday
journey
present
pretend
soldier
station

5 — ed, ing, s
crawl
creak
crowd
crown

6+ — ed, ing, s
expect
collect
correct
protect

6+ — ed, ing, s
repair
remain
remind
remember

7+ — ed, ing, s
disobey
discover
disappear
disappoint

112

You may add ing and s to the following words. You may not add ed. The words on the right of the columns are used instead.

buy	ing, s :	bought
lay	:	laid
pay	:	paid
say	:	said
cost	:	cost
feed	:	fed
feel	:	felt
find	:	found
hear	:	heard
hold	:	held

hurt	ing, s :	hurt
keep	:	kept
lead	:	led
lend	:	lent

wear	ing, s :	wore, worn
ring	:	rang, rung
sing	:	sang, sung
spring	:	sprang, sprung
sink	:	sank, sunk
drink	:	drank, drunk
think	:	thought
bring	:	brought
fight	:	fought
build	:	built

shoot	ing, s :	shot
sleep	:	slept
stand	:	stood
spend	:	spent

send		: sent
sell		: sold
tell		: told
meet		: met
mean		: meant
read		: read
see	n, ing, s	: saw
blow	n, ing, s	: blew
draw	n, ing, s	: drew
grow	n, ing, s	: grew
know	n, ing, s	: knew
throw	n, ing, s	: threw

sweep		: swept
swing		: swung
spread		: spread
break		: broke, n
speak		: spoke, n
steal		: stole, n
eat	en, ing, s	: ate
beat	en, ing, s	: beat
fall	en, ing, s	: fell
catch	ing, es	: caught
teach	ing, es	: taught

113

You may add ed, ing, es to all the following words

box	fish	kiss	fetch
fix ed, ing, es	dish ed, ing, es	miss ed, ing, es	match ed, ing, es
mix	push	cross	watch
	rush	pass	scratch
	wash	class	march
	wish	grass	reach
	brush	guess	bunch
	crash	press	lunch
	flash	dress	touch
	finish	address	search

All the following words end in a consonant followed by a letter **e**.
You may add **d** and **s** to all the words but the **e** must be dropped before adding ing, e.g.

hope   d, ~~e~~ing, s = **hoped, hoping, hopes**

4		4		4		5	
care	d, ~~e~~ing, s	dive	d, ~~e~~ing, s	hope	d, ~~e~~ing, s	argue	d, ~~e~~ing, s
dare		tire		rope		blame	
face		fire		note		flame	
race		wire		hole		place	
save		wipe		love		dance	
wave		fine		move		piece	
hate		line		name		force	
bake		live		side		voice	
rake		like		time		price	
wake		hike		type		prize	

~~e~~ Drop e before adding ing

continued on page 114

continued from page 113

5	d, eing, s		5	d, eing, s		6	d, eing, s		6	d, eing, s
chase			scare			battle			arrive	
close			score			bottle			behave	
cause			store			settle			chance	
pause			stone			bubble			bridge	
house			smile			paddle			change	
amuse			serve			puzzle			charge	
raise			taste			bundle			garage	
nurse			waste			hurdle			damage	
sense			brave			single			manage	
tease			prove						voyage	

6	d, eing, s		7	d, eing, s		7	d, eing, s		8	d, eing, s
decide			balance			picture			surprise	
divide			bandage			promise			exercise	
invite			believe			provide			exchange	
escape			bicycle			prepare			celebrate	
notice			breathe			produce			continue	
excuse			deserve			grumble			decorate	

refuse	capture	stumble	describe
rescue	explore	tremble	puncture
circle	imagine	trouble	struggle
centre	receive	whistle	treasure

All the words in the left-hand columns end in a consonant followed by a letter **e**. You may add s to all the words but the **e** must be dropped before adding ing.
You may not add d. The words on the right of the column are used instead.

come	e̸ing, s	: came	bite	e̸ing, s	: bit, bitten
make		: made	hide		: hid, hidden
lose		: lost	ride		: rode, ridden
leave		: left	rise		: rose, risen
slide		: slid	drive		: drove, driven
strike		: struck	write		: wrote, written
			choose		: chose, n

give	n, e̸ing, s	: gave
take	n, e̸ing, s	: took
shake	n, e̸ing, s	: shook
mistake	n, e̸ing, s	: mistook

e̸ Drop **e** before adding ing

115

You may add s to all the following words. The final consonant (the last letter) must be doubled before adding ed, ing, e.g.

drop ped, ping, s = **dropped, dropping, drops**

3	ted, ing, s	3	ped, ping, s	3	ged, ging, s	4	ped, ping, s
bat		**dip**		**beg**		**drop**	
pat		**rip**		**peg**		**chop**	
pet		**tip**		**gag**		**shop**	
net		**zip**		**wag**		**stop**	
wet		**hop**		**hug**		**swop**	
fit		**pop**		**tug**		**ship**	
rot		**top**		**gun**		**slip**	
rob		**tap**		**sun**		**skip**	
mob		**map**		**pin**		**drip**	
sob		**yap**		**jab**		**grip**	

4	ped, ping, s	4	ned, ning, s	5 +	led, ling, s	5 +	ted, ting, s
trip		**plan**		**equal**		**admit**	
whip		**stun**		**signal**		**permit**	

clap	grin	pencil	commit
snap	skin	model	regret
trap	skid	cancel	occur
wrap	chat	parcel	refer
step	plot	shovel	prefer
stab	knot	travel	equip
grab	knit	tunnel	kidnap
drag	dial	quarrel	unwrap

None of the following words may end in ed.
The words in the right-hand column are used instead.

get	ting, s : got	dig	ging, s : dug
set	ting, s : set	run	ning, s : ran
sit	ting, s : sat	win	ning, s : won
hit	ting, s : hit	spin	ning, s : spun
cut	ting, s : cut	begin	ning, s : began, begun
shut	ting, s : shut	swim	ming, s : swam, swum

116

You may add er, est, ly, ness to all the following words, e.g.
bolder, est, ly, ness = bolder, boldest, boldly, boldness

4	er, est, ly, ness	4+	er, est, ly, ness	5	er, est, ly, ness
bold		fair		light	
cold		dear		tight	
poor		near		quick	
cool		neat		quiet	
deep		mean		queer	
dark		weak		steep	
kind		clean		sharp	
loud		clear		short	
rich		cheap		smart	
slow		great		thick	
soft		fresh		rough	
wild		clever		tough	

You may add r, st, ly, ness to the following words:

4		4 +	
late	r, st, ly, ness	**rude**	r, st, ly, ness
nice		**wide**	
fine		**large**	
safe		**close**	
sore		**fierce**	
sure		**strange**	

You may add ly, ness to the following words but the last letter must be doubled before adding er, est.

3		3 +	
sad	der, dest, ly, ness	**fat**	ter; test
mad	der; dest	**flat**	ter; test
hot	ter; test	**thin**	ner; nest
fit	ter; test		

117

All the following words end in y.
The y must be dropped before adding ier, iest, ily, iness, e.g.

easy ier, iest, ily, iness = **easier, easiest, easily, easiness**

4 +		5	
easy	ier, iest, ily, iness	**happy**	ier, iest, ily, iness
lazy		**sunny**	
tidy		**funny**	
tiny		**fussy**	
ugly		**messy**	
dirty		**muddy**	
empty		**jolly**	
heavy		**silly**	
juicy		**sorry**	
lucky		**shaky**	
noisy		**weary**	
rocky		**windy**	

6

sticky	ier, iest, ily, iness
tricky	
shabby	
pretty	
lovely	
lonely	
sleepy	
greedy	
cheeky	
breezy	
gloomy	
stormy	

6+

hungry	ier, iest, ily, iness
cloudy	
clumsy	
chilly	
kindly	
steady	
untidy	
unlucky	
naughty	
thirsty	
healthy	
wealthy	

4+

busy	ier, iest, ily, iness
angry	ier, iest, ily
early	ier, iest, iness
merry	ier, iest, ily, iment

dough	also	Monday	January
cough	always	Tuesday	February
rough	almost	Wednesday	March
tough	although	Thursday	April
enough	already	Friday	May
plough	altogether	Saturday	June
through		Sunday	July
ought	all right		August
bought		spring	September
brought		summer	October
fought		autumn	November
thought		winter	December

All the following words end in **y**.
You may add ing but the **y** must be dropped before adding ied, ies.

cry	ing	**carry**	ing	**copy**	ing
cried	ies	**carried**	ies	**copied**	ies

dry **dried**	ing ies	**marry** **married**	ing ies	**bury** **buried**	ing ies
try **tried**	ing ies	**hurry** **hurried**	ing ies	**tidy** **tidied**	ing ies
fry **fried**	ing ies	**worry** **worried**	ing ies	**occupy** **occupied**	ing ies
spy **spied**	ing ies	**empty** **emptied**	ing ies	**satisfy** **satisfied**	ing ies
fly **flies** **flew, flown**	ing ies	**study** **studied**	ing ies	**terrify** **terrified**	ing ies

A very few verbs end in **ie**. You may add d and s but the **ie** must be changed to y before adding ing.

die **dying**	d, s	**lie** **lying**	d, s	**tie** **tying**	d, s

Singular	Plural
foot	feet
goose	geese
tooth	teeth
mouse	mice
man	men
woman	women
child	children
life	lives
wife	wives
knife	knives
leaf	leaves
loaf	loaves
thief	thieves
dwarf	s or dwarves

Singular	Plural
baby	ies
lady	ies
body	ies
pony	ies
city	ies
army	ies
navy	ies
aunty	ies
daddy	ies
mummy	ies
daisy	ies
dairy	ies
fairy	ies
story	ies
party	ies
jelly	ies

Singular	Plural
key	s
donkey	s
monkey	s
valley	s
chimney	s
cowboy	s
railway	s
gangway	s
holiday	s
birthday	s
zoo	s
piano	s
radio	s
hero	es
cargo	es

scarf	s or	scarves	lorry	ies	Negro	es
wharf	s or	wharves	puppy	ies	potato	es
hoof	s or	hooves	hobby	ies	tomato	es
roof	s		enemy	ies	volcano	es
elf		elves	canary	ies	bus	es
calf		calves	family	ies	glass	es
half		halves	granny	ies	beach	es
wolf		wolves	cherry	ies	peach	es
shelf		shelves	country	ies	torch	es
			library	ies	witch	es
self		selves	factory	ies	church	es
itself			robbery	ies	circus	es
myself			mystery	ies	princess	es
himself			discovery	ies	sandwich	es
herself						
yourself		yourselves	every	body, one, thing, where
		ourselves	any	body, one, thing, where, how, way
		themselves	some	body, one, thing, where, how, times

4		4		5		4		4		5	
able		than		these		bell		bird	s	giant	s
away		that		those		ball		desk	s	glove	s
best		then		where		wall		lake	s	green	s
born		them		which		hall		lawn	s	hedge	s
both		they		while		hill		lion	s	horse	s
does		this		whole		cake		neck	s	hotel	s
done		true		whose		card		nose	s	jewel	s
goes		luck		worse		cart		page	s	lemon	s
gone		ever		worst		cave		path	s	noise	s
gold		very		worth		case		pond	s	ocean	s

4		4		5		4		4		5	
dead		went		could		coal		shed	s	other	s
deaf		were		would		goal		shoe	s	owner	s
each		what		magic		door		sock	s	plate	s
else		when		might		food		song	s	fruit	s
just		with		money		moon		tent	s	pupil	s

					s		s
must	clay	music	room	town		purse	
much	beef	never	wood	tree		queen	
many	pork	pence	wool	mile		salad	
more	east	sugar	flag	your		shirt	
most	west	ready	frog	year		snake	

4	**5**	**5**	**4**	**5**		**5**	
from	about	among	game	apple	s	stair	s
next	above	below	gate	baker	s	stick	s
none	after	blood	gift	bread	s	stove	s
only	again	earth	hole	beast	s	sword	s
once	ahead	often	home	cabin	s	table	s
upon	alone	sorry	hour	cloth	s	thing	s
same	along	sheep	king	comic	s	tiger	s
some	alike	shall	kite	dozen	s	truck	s
soon	alive	under	knee	front	s	white	s
such	aside	until	idea	ghost	s	world	s

6		7		6		6		9	
across		against		friend		infant	s	adventure	s
afraid		another		forest		insect	s	aeroplane	s
around		because		finger		inside	s	afternoon	s
asleep		beneath		father		island	s	chocolate	s
ashore		between		mother		desert	s	favourite	s
awhile		clothes		leader		orange	s	passenger	s
before		instead		reader		second	s	newspaper	s
behind		nothing		saucer		minute	s	orchestra	s
better		perhaps		sister		moment	s	programme	s
cattle		without		reason		museum	s	vegetable	s

6		8		6		7			
during		together		bullet		bedroom	s	full	y
either		tomorrow		carrot		blanket	s	awful	ly
famous		horrible		coffee		brother	s	useful	ly
hardly		horribly		cotton		teacher	s	careful	ly
little		terrible		dinner		sausage	s	playful	ly
								cheerful	ly

middle
modern
unless
utmost
within

6
people
petrol
plenty
police
rather
really
safety
should
seldom
silver

terribly
possible
possibly
probable
probably

kitten s
lesson s
rabbit s
robber s
rubber s

6
animal s
banana s
beside s
bucket s
castle s
cousin s
coward s
danger s
engine s
needle s

parent s
person s
prince s
secret s
street s
string s
violin s
window s
pillow s
yellow s

cabbage s
cottage s
message s
village s
lettuce s

7
chicken s
kitchen s
husband s
pudding s
morning s
evening s
tadpole s
tractor s
visitor s
outside s

dreadful ly
thankful ly
beautiful ly
forgetful ly
wonderful ly

helpful s
hopeful s
skilful s
faithful s
grateful s
peaceful s
powerful s
spiteful s
delightful s
disgraceful ly

122

Homophones

These are words that sound alike but have different meanings and spellings.

arc curve
ark boat; box
beach seashore
beech tree
bean plant
been past of be
blew blow
blue colour
bough branch
bow bend
brake to stop
break to snap
chute a slide
shoot fire
die lose life
dye colour

pain suffering
pane of glass
pair two
pear fruit
peace quiet
piece a part
peer stare
pier jetty
place position
plaice fish
rap knock
wrap cover
sail ship
sale selling
slay kill
sleigh sled

accept receive
except leaving out
allowed let; permitted
aloud loudly
altar church table
alter change
dear beloved; costly
deer animal
flour ground wheat
flower blossom
foul dirty; unfair
fowl bird
freeze ice; cold
frieze wall decoration
groan moan
grown got bigger

farther further
father parent
fort castle
fought fight
hair of head
hare animal
hart stag
heart of body
heal cure
heel of foot
higher taller
hire rent
hoarse husky
horse animal
leant leaned
lent lend
made make
maid girl
muscle of body
mussel shellfish

stair step
stare look at
steal thieve
steel metal
tail end
tale story
pail bucket
pale whitish
scene view; place
seen noticed
tire weary
tyre wheel cover
weak not strong
week seven days
weather climate
whether if
wood timber
would past of will
won did win
one single

guessed did guess
guest visitor
hear listen
here in this place
heard listened
herd of cattle, etc.
hoard hidden store
horde crowd
hour sixty minutes
our belonging to us
hole hollow place
whole all; complete
meat flesh
meet come together
meter measuring box
metre length measure
moan groan
mown cut grass, etc.
signet seal, ring
cygnet young swan

knew know
new just made
knight Sir
night opp. of day
know understand
no not any; opp. of yes
knot tied string, etc.
not no
passed did pass
past time gone by
ring circle; bell sound
wring twist
wait stay; serve
weight heaviness
way direction
weigh measure heaviness
waste not used; useless
waist of body

shore seashore
sure certain
their belonging to them
there in that place
they're they are
theirs belonging to them
there's there is
threw throw
through from end to end
throne king's seat
thrown throw
board wood; go on ship; lodge
bored weary; drilled hole
cereal wheat, oats, etc.
serial in parts
currant fruit
current flow of water, air, etc.
cue hint; billiard-stick

which what one? who?
witch old woman
who's who is
whose belonging to whom?
you're you are
your belonging to you
it's it is
its belonging to it
pedal foot lever
peddle to hawk goods
hall room; passage
haul pull; amount taken
him he
hymn song of praise
mare female horse
mayor head of town or city
medal badge – for bravery, etc.
meddle interfere
pray ask God
prey victim; thing hunted

queue line of persons, etc.
fair just; light; entertainment
fare price of journey; food
core middle of apple, etc.
corps group of cadets, etc.
road highway
rode ride
rowed used oars
cent coin
sent send
scent smell; perfume
rain water
reign rule
rein strap
buy purchase
by near to, etc.
bye a run
to towards
too also; more than enough
two number

Index

Oxford University Press, Walton Street, Oxford, OX2 6DP

Oxford New York

Athens Auckland Bangkok Bombay Calcutta Cape Town
Dar es Salaam Delhi Florence Hong Kong Istanbul Karachi
Kuala Lumpur Madras Madrid Melbourne Mexico City Nairobi
Paris Singapore Taipei Tokyo Toronto

and associated companies in
Berlin Ibadan

Oxford is a trade mark of Oxford University Press

First published in paperback 1962
Second edition in paperback 1981
First published in hardback 1992
First published in Mini format 1995

10 9 8 7 6 5 4 3 2 1

ISBN 0 19 910357 7

A CIP catalogue record for this book is available from the British Library

Printed in Great Britain by Butler & Tanner Limited, Frome and London